On the Map USA

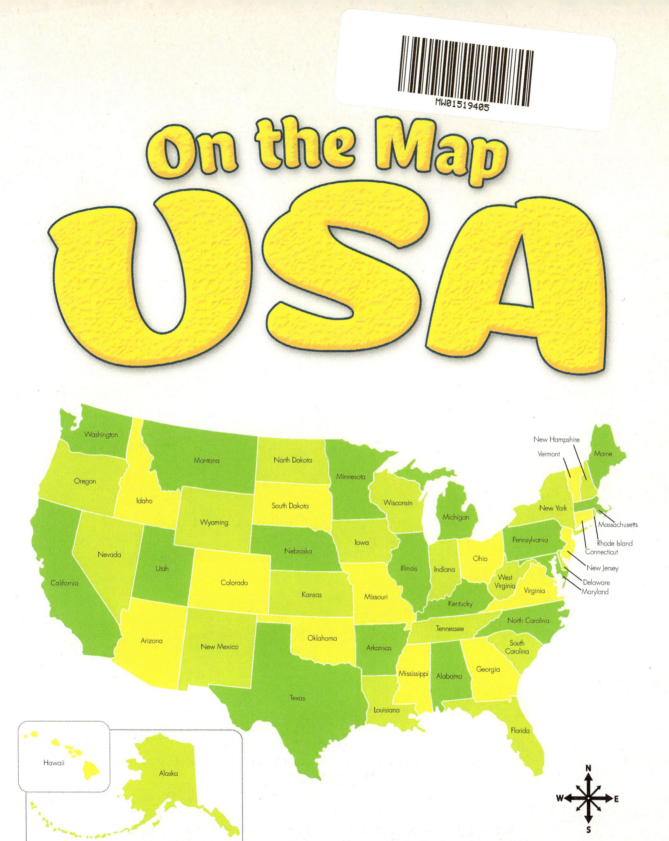

DOVER PUBLICATIONS, INC.
MINEOLA, NEW YORK

Bibliographical Note

On the Map: USA, first published by Dover Publications, Inc., in 2015, contains pages
from the following online workbooks published by Education.com: *Reading for Information:*
U.S. Cities, Reading for Information: U.S. Cities 2, Learn the 50 States, and *U.S. Capitals.*

International Standard Book Number

ISBN-13: 978-0-486-80266-4
ISBN-10: 0-486-80266-3

Manufactured in the United States by Courier Corporation
80266301   2015
www.doverpublications.com

CONTENTS

READING FOR INFORMATION:

U.S. Cities

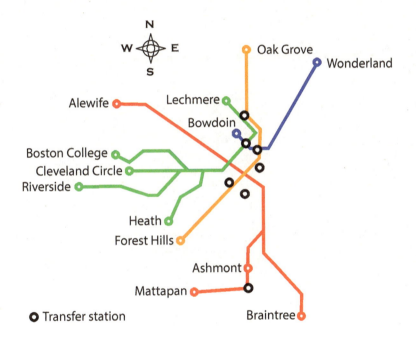

The history of... *Boston*

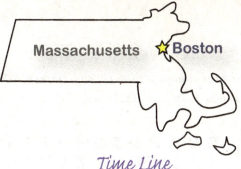

Massachusetts ⭐ **Boston**

Time Line

1630
Puritan colonists establish Boston.

1636
Harvard is opened.

late 1700s
The American Revolution takes place, and Boston is the site of many famous acts of rebellion.

1800s
Irish immigrants begin to settle in Boston.

1872
The Great Boston Fire damages about 65 acres of the city.

2004
The Boston Red Sox win their first world series in 86 years.

Word Search!

Find the famous landmarks and features listed below.
Words may be forward, backward, diagonal, or upside down.

```
F R N Z Y T I C Y D N I W
R A L W L N S Z L R O M X
O M N R I C A N U I Z E O
B A K E D B E A N S C I S
N N D O U U E O A E B S D
M D I U Z I B X O R M D E
U L R A T M L Z A B A A R
S F B J I P G H O O T Y N
E Z R X L R S L A A A N O
U O E E I V C G E L O L T
M H W X N I I Z N S L B S
C H A R L E S R I V E R O
S C I T L E C N O T S O B
```

Faneuil Hall
Boston Red Sox
Charles River
Baked Beans
Boston Celtics

Research

Fill in the blank:
Boston Harbor has 34 _islands_
peninsula

Ride the *subway!*

Boston's underground transit system, "The T," was the first active subway in the United States. Can you find your way to the stations below? Using the subway map for clues, fill in the blanks with the line color or station name.

1. To get from Forest Hills station to Oak Grove station, take the _____ line.
2. To get from Lechmere station to Heath station, take the _____ line.
3. To get from Alewife station to Mattapan station, take the Red Line and transfer at _____ station.

N W E S

Oak Grove
Wonderland
Alewife
Lechmere
Bowdoin
Boston College
Cleveland Circle
Riverside
Heath
Forest Hills
Ashmont
Mattapan
⊙ Transfer station
Braintree

The history of...

Washington, D.C.

District of
Columbia

Maryland

Washington, D.C.

Virginia

Word Search!

*Find the famous landmarks and features listed below.
Words may be forward, backward, diagonal, or upside down.*

```
S C A P I T O L H I L L Y
N I L W L N L Z L N O I P
U C I O D S T A S I E A H
P O T O M A C R I V E R C
X N E O H U I O A A B O E
I D P U Z E T X O U M R Q
N L C A T M N Z A T A T E
E F W H I T E H O U S E W
O Z R X L R E L R Z A M D
H O D E I V T F E K O L K
K E N N E D Y C E N T E R
A T Z F N O I J O N E A B
E R A U Q N R E E B O I P
```

Metrorail
White House
Capitol Hill
Potomac River
Kennedy Center

Time Line

1791

The U.S. capital is
moved from
Philadelphia to D.C.

1814

1865

Lincoln is assassinated
at Ford's Theater.

British troops set
fire to the Capitol
building and the
White House during
the War of 1812.

1901

1963

The National Mall
is redesigned.

The March on
Washington takes place
on the National Mall.

Research

How is Washington, D.C., different from
all other U.S. states?

————

Connect the dots!

Can you guess which memorial
structure is pictured here?
Connect the dots to find out!

The history of... *Detroit*

Michigan

⭐ Detroit

Word Search!

Find and circle the famous features listed below.
Words may be forward, backward, diagonal, or upside down.

```
D E T R O I T T I G E R S
E S L W L N S Z L N O M P
T C L O D S R A S I E N H
R B X L V E A D T M C I C
O N E O U U E O A A B S E
I D P U Z B B X O U M G Q
T L C A T M O Z A T A N E
R F H J I P G G O A T I W
I Z R X L R A M O T O W N
V O D E I V C F E C O D K
E H O X N I I Z O N I E E
R T Z F N O H J O N E R B
L Q Z E Y T I C R O T O M
```

Motor City
Detroit Tigers
Red Wings
Motown
Detroit River

Time Line

1701

A trading post called Fort Pontchartrain du Detroit is established.

1802

Detroit is incorporated as a town.

1850s

Detroit is the last stop on the Underground Railroad because it is so close to Canada.

1899

Henry Ford builds his factory in Detroit.

1960

Music producer Berry Gordy founds Motown Records.

Research

Fill in the blank:
Detroit is the _____ city in the state of Michigan.

_____

Spot the Differences!

Detroit's famous nickname is "The Motor City," for its famous spot in automobile manufacturing history. Can you find five differences between these two cars? You can color them, too!

The history of... *Chicago*

Illinois

Chicago

Word Search!

Find the famous landmarks and features listed below.
Words may be forward, backward, diagonal, or upside down.

```
S O N Z Y T I C Y D N I W
N S L W L N S Z L N O M P
K C L O D S R A S I E N H
R B X L V E A D T M C I C
A N E O U U E O A A B S E
P D P U Z B B X O U M D Q
N L C A T M O Z A T A A E
L F H J I P G G O A T Y W
O Z R X L R A L A Z A N D
C O D E I V C F E C O L K
N H O X N I I Z O N I B E
I T Z F N O H J O N E H B
L A K E M I C H I G A N C
```

Lincoln Park
Lake Michigan
Chicago Bears
Chicago Bulls
Windy City

Time Line

1781
Explorer Jean Baptiste du Sable settles the area.

1871
The Great Fire destroys the city.

1892
The first El train runs.

1893
The World Columbian Exposition is held.

1908
The FBI establishes its Chicago offices.

1973
The Sears Tower is opened.

Research

How did Chicago get its name?

_____

Name that *lake!*

Chicago sits on Lake Michigan, one of the Great Lakes.
Can you match the Great Lakes with their names?

A) Lake Superior
B) Lake Huron
C) Lake Michigan
D) Lake Ontario
E) Lake Erie

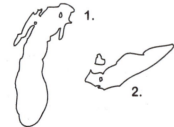

1.
2.
3.
4.
5.

The history of... *Cleveland*

★ **Cleveland**

Ohio

Time Line

1796

Surveyors map the land and name it after the project's leader, Moses Cleaveland.

1870

John D. Rockefeller founds Standard Oil in Cleveland.

1830s

Cleveland begins to grow after completion of nearby Erie Canal.

late 1800s - mid-1900s

For almost a century, Cleveland is a major center of industry for products like oil, steel, and automobiles.

1995

The Rock and Roll Hall of Fame opens.

Word Search!

Find the famous landmarks and features listed below. Words may be forward, backward, diagonal, or upside down.

```
B O N Z Y T I C Y D N I C
R R V I R I R U O S S I U
I C O O D S R A S I E N Y
S B X W V E A D T M C I A
H N E O N U E O A A B S H
M D P U Z S L H O U M D O
U L C A T M A I A T A A G
S F H J I P K A O A T B A
E Z R X L R E R R Z A O R
U O P E N G E I N M O T I
M H O X N I R V O N V Z Z
R A Z I N D I A N S X Z E
C A V A L I E R S D G E R
```

Cuyahoga River
Lake Erie
Indians
Cavaliers
Browns

Spot the *differences!*

Famous guitar designer Les Paul created many of the guitars on display at the Rock and Roll Hall of Fame and Museum. Perhaps his most famous guitar is one called the Gibson Les Paul, used by many of the most famous rock and roll players in history. Find five differences between the Les Paul Gibson at right and the guitar on the left. Then, color them in!

Research

Cleveland's first resident was a settler named _____ .

_____

The history of...

Kansas City

Kansas City ★
Missouri

Word Search!

Find the famous landmarks and features listed below.
Words may be forward, backward, diagonal, or upside down.

```
I O N Z Y T I C Y D N I W
R E V I R I R U O S S I M
I C L O D S R A S I E N H
S B X L V E A D T M C I C
H N E O U U E O A A B S E
M D P U Z B B X O U M D Q
U L C A T M C Z A T A A E
S F H J I P H G O A T R W
E Z R X L R I L A Z A O D
U O D E I V E F E C O Y K
M H O X N I F Z O N I A E
J A Z Z F E S T I V A L B
Z A K V M I C B I G A S C
```

Missouri River
Irish Museum
Jazz Festival
Chiefs
Royals

Time Line

1833

John Calvin McCoy starts a trading post.

1838

The "Town of Kansas" is established.

1854 - 1858

A fight takes place in the Kansas Territory between pro- and anti-slavery groups, which leads to the Civil War.

1908

Henry Perry begins selling barbecue from a street corner. His recipe becomes the "Kansas City" style of barbecue.

1922

Walt Disney founds Laugh-O-Gram Studios in Kansas City.

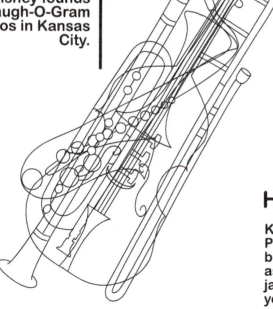

Research

Kansas City has the second-highest number of _____ of any city in the world.

_____

How many *instruments?*

Kansas City earned the nickname "Paris of the Plains" during the jazz age, from 1920 - 1940. It became a center of jazz and other music, as well as literature, arts, and performance. How many jazz instruments can you find in this picture? Can you name them all?

The history of... *Miami*

Florida

Miami

Time Line

early 1800s

Settlers begin to move into the area.

late 1800s

Local woman Julia Tuttle convinces railroad companies to build a line to Miami. She succeeds, the city grows, and it is founded in 1896.

1910s

Miami's becomes a top tourist destination.

1926

The Great Miami Hurricane hits land.

1960s

Cuban immigrants begin to settle in Miami.

Word Search!

Find the famous landmarks and people listed below. Words may be forward, backward, diagonal, or upside down.

```
F O F D C Z O O O A O P M
C R L W L N L Z L N O M I
A P E S U V C T E R G B A
N B X N V E H D T M C I M
A N E O C U I O A A B S I
L D R A G H F G A R G C D
S L C A T M Q Z A D A A O
T F H J I P T U O I T Y L
C O R A L R E E F S A N P
E B M O V P W E P R B E H
E I U A D A N A T A T B I
A T L A N T I C O C E A N
J A F Z B U Z I C A O Y S
```

Biscayne Bay
Miami Dolphins
Atlantic Ocean
Port of Miami
Coral Reefs

Research

Fill in the blank:

Miami is the only city in the United States to lie between two _____.

_____

How many starfish?

Florida's beaches are home to many exotic sea creatures, including the starfish! How many starfish can you find in the drawing on the left? Once you find the answer, color the drawing however you like!

The history of... *Houston*

Texas

Houston

Time Line

1836
Two real estate developers establish Houston.

1846
Texas joins the union.

1861
Houston votes to secede, and is readmitted in 1870.

1963
NASA opens its Houston research and flight control center.

2005
Hurricane Katrina evacuees take shelter in Houston's AstroDome.

Word Search!

Find the famous landmarks and features listed below.
Words may be forward, backward, diagonal, or upside down.

```
H O U S T O N R O D E O S
O I L W L N L Z L N O M E
U P M S U V C T E R L B E
S B X I V E H D T E C I R
T N E O H U I O N A B S T
O D P U G Z T N O U N D A
N L C A T M A Z A D A A I
A F H J I H T D O I T Y L
S Z R X C R E L R S A N O
T B M P V P W E P I B E N
R I I A D A N A T A X B G
O H Z F N T I J O C E A A
S P A C E C E N T E R A M
```

Houston Astros
Magnolia Trees
Space Center
Ship Channel
Houston Rodeo

Word Scramble!

Houston has played an important role in space travel through NASA (the National Aeronautics and Space Administration), earning it the nickname of "Space City." Unscramble these words to learn some interesting facts about Houston and space exploration!

Research

Houston is different from all other Texas cities in what way?

_____

Color the
Space Shuttle!

1. Houston is home to NASA _____ , which directs NASA space flights.
2. It controls the U.S. part of the International _____ .

ISONSIM LTROCON

CEPSA ONTATSI

The history of... *Albuquerque*

Albuquerque ★

New Mexico

Time Line

1706
Albuquerque is founded as a Spanish outpost on the Camino Real.

1862
Albuquerque is surrendered to the South during the Civil War.

1926
Route 66 is opened.

1972
The first Balloon Fiesta is held.

1975
Microsoft is founded in Albuquerque.

Word Search!

Find the famous landmarks and features listed below.
Words may be forward, backward, diagonal, or upside down.

```
H O T A I R B A L L O O N
R S L W L I S Z L X O L P
E M E R I O A N R I V D R
R B G L V G A D T Z C T C
T N D O U R E O A E B O E
A D I U Z A B X O R M W Q
E L R A T N N Z A U A N E
H F B J I D G W O O T Y W
T Z R X Z E N A O A A N D
O O E E I V C G E M O L K
M H W E S T M E S A D B E
I T O F N O H J O I E L B
K X T E M I C B I G K N O
```

Old Town
Rio Grande
Hot Air Balloon
West Mesa
KiMo Theater

Research

The word "KiMo" means "mountain lion" in what language?

_____

What are *petroglyphs?*

Petroglyphs are pictures etched into the surface of rocks. The ones at Petroglyph National Monument in Albuquerque date as far back as the 1300s! They described the complex society and religion of the Pueblo Indians who drew them. Can you match the petroglyphs on the rocks below with their meanings? *Optional*: Turn your paper over and draw your own petroglyph "story!"

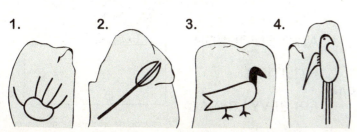

1.   2.   3.   4.

A. *Macaw bird*. Since Macaws were not native, this may be evidence of trade with Central and South American peoples.

B. *Unknown bird*. Birds are often represented in petroglyphs.

C. *Yucca pod*. Represents the importance of land cultivation.

D. *A hand*. A single hand is one of the most common petroglyphs.

The history of... *Portland*

★ Portland

Oregon

Word Search!

Find the famous landmarks and features listed below.
Words may be forward, backward, diagonal, or upside down.

```
J C O F Z X E B H O R S S
C O L U M B I A R I V E R
A P R S U V C T E R G B E
N B X E V H D T M R I Z
A N E O G U I O A A E S A
L D P U G O T S O U E D L
S L C A T M N Z A D N A B
T F H J I P T Z O I C Y L
C O R A L R E E O S I N I
E B M O V P W E P O T E A
E I U A D A N A T A Y B R
A T Z F N T I J O C E A T
E S K O O B S L L E W O P
```

Columbia River
Trail Blazers
Oregon Zoo
Powell's Books
Green City

Time Line

1805
Lewis and Clark reach the Portland area.

1851
Portland becomes a city.

1840s
Portland is a small stopping point along the Willamette River.

late 1800s
Portland is now 2nd largest city on the West coast.

late 1990s –'00s
Artists and musicians begin to move into Portland, and it becomes a city known for its creative culture.

Research

Portland is also known by what flower-related nickname?

_____

Color the famous *Portlandia statue!*

Portlandia by artist Raymond Kaskey

Fill in the blanks!

Portland is home to a great variety of art and artists. Can you unscramble the answers to these questions about Portland art, literature and film?

1. Portland is home to *The Simpsons* animator _____.

2. _____ is a movie recently filmed in Portland.

3. _____ , author of the *Ramona Quimby* books, grew up in Portland.

ATMT ENIOGNGR

HTILITWG

ERLBEVY LRYEAC

The history of...
San Francisco

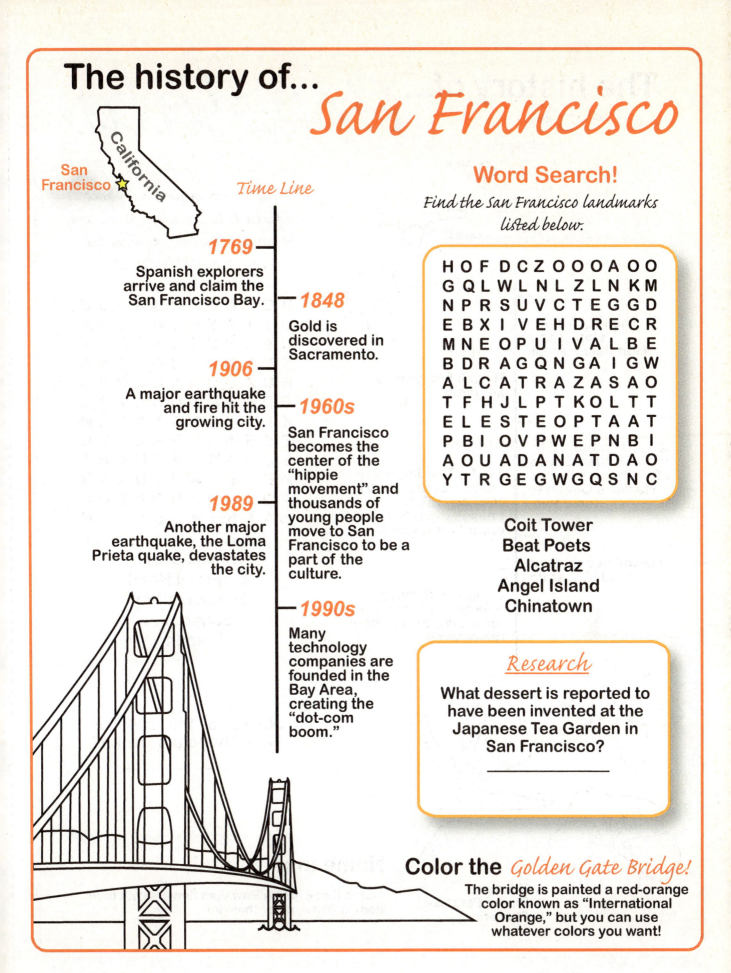

California

San Francisco

Time Line

1769
Spanish explorers arrive and claim the San Francisco Bay.

1848
Gold is discovered in Sacramento.

1906
A major earthquake and fire hit the growing city.

1960s
San Francisco becomes the center of the "hippie movement" and thousands of young people move to San Francisco to be a part of the culture.

1989
Another major earthquake, the Loma Prieta quake, devastates the city.

1990s
Many technology companies are founded in the Bay Area, creating the "dot-com boom."

Word Search!
Find the San Francisco landmarks listed below.

```
H O F D C Z O O O A O O
G Q L W L N L Z L N K M
N P R S U V C T E G G D
E B X I V E H D R E C R
M N E O P U I V A L B E
B D R A G Q N G A I G W
A L C A T R A Z A S A O
T F H J L P T K O L T T
E L E S T E O P T A A T
P B I O V P W E P N B I
A O U A D A N A T D A O
Y T R G E G W G Q S N C
```

Coit Tower
Beat Poets
Alcatraz
Angel Island
Chinatown

Research
What dessert is reported to have been invented at the Japanese Tea Garden in San Francisco?

_____

Color the *Golden Gate Bridge!*
The bridge is painted a red-orange color known as "International Orange," but you can use whatever colors you want!

The history of... *Honolulu*

Kauai

Hawaii

Oahu

Honolulu ☆

Molokai

Lanai

Maui

Big Island

Time Line

1794

The first foreign ship enters Honolulu Harbor.

1810

Hawaii becomes a kingdom.

1893

Hawaii is annexed by the United States after the U.S. forces Hawaii's Queen to step down.

1941

1941 – The Japanese military bombs Pearl Harbor, which causes the U.S. to enter World War II.

1959

Hawaii becomes an official U.S. state.

1993

Congress formally apologizes to Hawaii for overthrowing their government.

Word Search!

Find the Honolulu landmarks and features listed below. Words may be forward, backward, diagonal, or even upside down!

```
D O F D C Z O U O A O G
G I T T Y M U N E U M A
N P A S U V C I D G G Y
S M A M S I U O L T S A
H O Z D O N A C L O V B
B D R A G N D S A I G A
X L C X O R D T A S A M
T F H W L P E H L L T U
S U G A R C A N E A A A
P B I S L A N I D A A N
A O U A D A N O A D D A
W A I K I K I B E A C H
```

Waikiki Beach
Diamond Head
Hanauma Bay
Sugarcane
Volcano

Research

What does the Hawaiian word "honolulu" mean?

_____

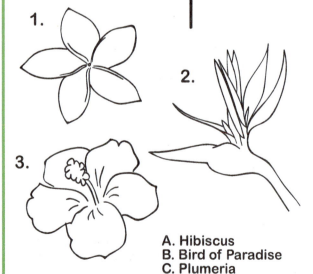

1.

2.

3.

A. Hibiscus
B. Bird of Paradise
C. Plumeria

Name that *flower!*

Match these native Hawaiian flowers with their names. Then, color them in!

Great job!

_____

is an Education.com reading superstar

READING FOR INFORMATION:

U.S. Cities 2

The history of... New York

New York

New York City

Word Search!

Find the famous landmarks and features listed below.
Words may be forward, backward, diagonal, or upside down.

Time Line

1609

Henry Hudson explores the area that would become New York City.

1788

New York City is made the capital of the U.S.

1776-1777

General George Washington and his troops fight the New York Campaign of the American Revolution.

1920s

The Harlem Renaissance occurs in New York's African-American community.

1886

Statue of Liberty is dedicated.

2001

Almost 3,000 people die in the terrorist attacks on the Twin Towers.

1951

The U.N. moves to Manhattan.

```
S R N Z Y Z I C Y S N I N
L T L W L N S Z L C O M E
V M O R I C A N R E V E W
I B G C R E A D T N C I A
S N D O K I E O A T B S M
P D I U Z E V X O R M D S
R L R A T M X E A A A A T
E F B J I P G C R L T Y E
S Z R X Y D N A H P W N R
L O E B R O A D W A Y L D
E H W X N I I Z N R N T A
Y T O F N O H J O K E G M
L X T I M E S S Q U A R E
```

New Amsterdam
Broadway
Times Square
Central Park
Stock Exchange

Research

What island, located in New York Bay, belongs in part to New York City and in part to Jersey City, New Jersey?

_____

Name that *borough!*

A borough is an area with its own government, usually within a city. New York City is made up of five boroughs. Can you match the name of the borough with its place on the map?

A. Manhattan
B. Brooklyn
C. Queens
D. Staten Island
E. Bronx

1. _____
2. _____
3. _____
4. _____
5. _____

The history of... *Pittsburgh*

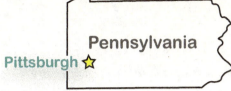

Pennsylvania

Pittsburgh ⭐

Word Search!

Find the famous landmarks and features listed below. Words may be forward, backward, diagonal, or upside down.

```
P O N Z Y T I C Y D N I W
R I V I R I R U O S S I M
I C R O D S R A S I E N H
S B X A V E A D T M C I C
H N E O T U E O A A B S E
M D P U Z E B H O U M D S
U L C A T M S I A T A A R
S F H J I P H O O A T B E
E Z R X L R I R A Z A O L
U O P E N G U I N S O T E
M H O X N I F V O N I Z E
R A Z T F E B E I V X L T
C I T Y O F B R I D G E S
```

Ohio River
City of Bridges
Pirates
Steelers
Penguins

Time Line

1700s
Traders begin to settle in the area.

mid-1800s
After rebuilding, Pittsburgh becomes a leading industrial city, producing steel and coal.

1845
The Great Fire of Pittsburgh burns the city.

1950s
Jonas Salk develops polio vaccine at University of Pittsburgh.

1936
The St. Patrick's Day flood hits.

1980s
Pittsburgh becomes a hub for medical technology and services.

Research

Pittsburgh lies at the meeting point of the _____ and _____ Rivers.

_____

Name that *bridge!*

Pittsburgh has more bridges than any other state in the U.S. Match the bridges below with their names. Then, color them in!

1.

2.

3.

A. California Avenue Bridge
B. 10th Street Bridge
C. Smithfield Street Bridge

The history of... *Minneapolis*

Minnesota

Minneapolis ⭐

Word Search!

Find the famous landmarks and features listed below.
Words may be forward, backward, diagonal, or upside down.

```
T W I N S V I C H I L L Y
U I L W L N L Z L N O C P
N E M A D S T A S I E I H
I X T B B A C R I V E T C
O T E O E A I O A A B Y E
N E P U Z R M X O U M O Q
S R C A T M W A A T A F E
T A W H R I V O R W A L K
A V R X L R E L L I A A D
T E D E Y V T F E V V K K
V I K I N G S R E T E E D
O U Z F X O I J O N E S R
N E A U Q N R E E B O I P
```

City of Lakes
Timberwolves
Twins
Vikings
Lynx

Time Line

1680
French explorers arrive.

1819
The army builds Fort Snelling.

1867
Minneapolis is incorporated as a city.

late 1800s
Factories are built around the waterfalls to take advantage of hydropower.

1934
Factory workers hold a protest against working conditions, and fair labor laws are passed as a result.

1952
Major advancements in open-heart surgery technology are made at the University of Minnesota.

Research

The name "Minneapolis" combines words from what two languages?

———

Solve the *maze!*

The Minneapolis park system is one of the best in the U.S. Can you find your way from one end of the Chain of Lakes to the other? Don't fall in the lake!

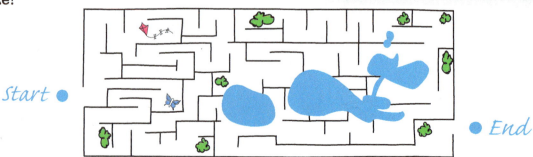

Start ●

● *End*

The history of... *Baltimore*

Maryland
★ **Baltimore**

Time Line

1706
The Port of Baltimore is opened.

1729
Baltimore is founded.

1776
For a few months during the American Revolution, the nation's capital is moved to Baltimore.

1814
The Battle at Fort McHenry inspires Francis Scott Key to write "The Star-Spangled Banner."

1904
The Great Baltimore Fire destroys 70 blocks of the city.

1968
Riots break out in Baltimore after the assassination of Dr. Martin Luther King, Jr.

Word Search!

Find the famous landmarks and people listed below.
Words may be forward, backward, diagonal, or upside down.

```
F O F D C Z O O O A O H
O Q L W L N L Z L N K T
R P R E U V C T E G G U
T B X S V E H D R E C R
M N E U P U I M A L B E
C D R O G Q U G A I G B
H L C H T I A Z A S A A
E F H G R P T K O L T B
N L E A T E O P T A A T
R B U L V P W E P N B I
Y Q U F D A N A T D A O
A O R I O L E P A R K C
```

Oriole Park
Aquarium
Fort McHenry
Flag House
Babe Ruth

Research

What kind of craft was successfully launched in Baltimore for the first time in U.S. history?

_____

Spot the Differences!

The Preakness Stakes is a thoroughbred horse race run each year in May. Can you find 5 differences between these race horses?

The history of...

Missouri ⭐ St. Louis

St. Louis

Word Search!

Find the St. Louis landmarks and features listed below. Words may be forward, backward, diagonal, or even upside down!

Time Line

1764

Pierre LaClede and his partner Auguste Chouteau establish a settlement on the banks of the Mississippi River.

1803

The U.S. acquires St. Louis as part of the Louisiana Purchase.

1804

The Lewis and Clark Expedition leaves St. Louis.

1846

The *Scott v. Emerson* case takes place in the Old Courthouse.

1904

St. Louis hosts the Louisiana Purchase Exposition and the Summer Olympics.

1967

The Gateway Arch is opened.

```
H O F D C Z O U O A O G
G E T T Y M U N E U M A
N P R S U V C I D G G T
S M A R S I U O L T S E
H O Z D Y W G N D L B W
B D R A G T D S A I G A
X L C X O R G T A S A Y
T F H W L P E A L L T A
E L N S T E R T I A A R
P B I S L A N I D R A C
A O U A D A N O A D A H
Y V E N I C E N E A C H
```

Gateway Arch
Union Station
Dogtown
Cardinals
St. Louis Rams

Research

The St. Louis area is home to a park, animal farm, and historical site named for what U.S. President?

_____

Spot the *differences!*

On the Tree Walk at Forest Park, you can see 90 different types of trees! Find five differences between these trees. You can even color them in!

The history of... *New Orleans*

Time Line

late 1600s — French explorers and traders arrive.

1763 — New Orleans comes under Spanish rule as a result of the Seven Years' War.

1718 — New Orleans is founded by the French.

1800 — Spain gives Louisiana back to France.

1803 — The U.S. acquires the Louisiana Territory from France.

1897 — Free man Homer Plessy is arrested for refusing to ride in the segregated car on a train passing through New Orleans.

2005 — Hurricane Katrina, the largest and most destructive storm to hit the city, hits land.

New Orleans

Word Search!

Find the New Orleans landmarks and features listed below. Words may be forward, backward, diagonal, or even upside down!

```
F O F D C Z O O O A O O F
C R L W L N L Z L N K M G
A P E S U V C T E G G D N
N B X N V E H D R M C R A
A N E O C U I V A A B E Y
L D R A G H N G A R G W A
S L C A T R Q Z A D A O L
T F H J L P T U O I T T A
R L R Z S B A N A G A T B
E B I O V P W E P R B I M
E O U A D A N A T A T O A
T T R G E G W G Q S N E J
J A Z Z M U S I C A O O R
```

French Quarter
Jambalaya
Jazz Music
Canal Street
Mardi Gras

Research

What did the French originally name New Orleans, and what did the name mean?

_____

Give yourself *Mardi Gras beads!*

Mardi Gras is an annual celebration that falls on "Fat Tuesday," a part of the holiday of Lent. Colorful beads of all shapes and sizes are a fun part of the Mardi Gras celebration. Draw your portrait in the space provided, then color the beads and draw some of your own--as many as you like!

The history of... *Montgomery*

Alabama
⭐ Montgomery

Word Search!

*Find the famous landmarks and features listed below.
Words may be forward, backward, diagonal, or upside down.*

```
R A W L I V I C H I L L Y
U D L W L N L Z L N O I P
N E A A D S T A S I E A H
I X T G B A C R I V E R C
O T E O A A I O A A B O E
N E P U Z Q M X O U M R Q
S R C A T M A A A T A T E
T A W H R I V E R W A L K
A V R X L R E L I I A M D
T E D E I V T F E N V L K
I N N N E D Y R E T X E D
O U Z F N O I J O N E R R
N E A U Q N R E E B O I P
```

Alabama River
Union Station
Riverwalk
Dexter Avenue
Civil War

Time Line

1819

Montgomery is incorporated.

1861

The order for the attack on Fort Sumter issued from the new capital.

During the Civil War, Montgomery is made the capital of the Confederacy.

1910

The Wright Brothers begin to establish flying schools and airfields in Montgomery. One later becomes Maxwell-Gunter Air Force Base.

1950s – 1960s

Montgomery is a hotbed of Civil Rights activism. The Montgomery Bus Boycott and the Selma to Montgomery March both take place in town.

1963

The March on Washington takes place on the National Mall.

Research

Montgomery was the first U.S. city to have a city-wide _____ system.

_____

Guide the *Montgomery marchers!*

The Selma to Montgomery Marches helped make it illegal to block African Americans from registering to vote. Can you guide these demonstrators on their way? Help them find a path from the city of Selma to Montgomery.

Selma ○

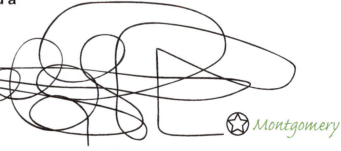

⭐ *Montgomery*

The history of...
Nashville

Nashville ☆
Tennessee

Word Search!

Find the famous landmarks and features listed below. Words may be forward, backward, diagonal, or upside down.

```
R A D N O R L A K E O F C
X I L W C N O Z G N O R O
A O M S I C N A R O G A U
H S Z N S N C B A X F N N
A N E N U C I S N A S C T
L D P U T E N S D U O I R
S L C A T R B Z O D K S Y
T F H J I P O D L I C N M
C Z R X L R W M E S I A U
E B M O V P L E O I H S S
S R E G N A R S P S D H I
A T Z F N T I J R C I A C
M U S I C C I T Y N O P T
```

Music City
Radnor Lake
Grand Ole Opry
Francis Nash
Country Music

Time Line

1779
James Robertson settles the area.

early 1800s
Nashville resident Andrew Jackson becomes a war hero for his actions in the War of 1812 and brings attention to the town.

1861
Tennessee secedes from the Union.

1941
The country's first FM radio station begins broadcasting out of Nashville.

1950s
Country music production becomes a major industry.

Research

A copy of the ancient Greek structure, the _____, stands in Nashville's Centennial Park.

_____

Name that *instrument!*

Nashville is known for country music, which uses many of its own unique instruments. Match the instruments below with their names. Then, color them in!

1.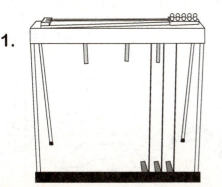

2.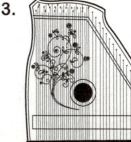

3.

A. Dobro

B. Zither

C. Pedal Steel Guitar

25

The history of... *Phoenix*

Arizona
★ Phoenix

Word Search!

Find the famous landmarks and features listed below.
Words may be forward, backward, diagonal, or upside down.

```
S O N O R A N D E S E R T
N I L W L N L Z L N O M P
U N I O N S T A T I O N H
S B X I V E H D T M C I C
X N E O H U I O A A B S E
I D P U Z E T X O U M D Q
N L C A T M N Z A T A A E
E F H J I P T D O A T Y W
O Z R X L R E L R Z A N D
H O L E I N T H E R O C K
P H O E N I X Z O O X B E
A T Z F N O I J O N E A B
E R A U Q N R E E B O I P
```

Sonoran Desert
Phoenix Suns
Hole-In-The-Rock
Phoenix Zoo
Union Station

Time Line

1860s

Explorer Jack Swilling finds ruins of an ancient civilization in the White Tank Mountains and decides to rebuild it. Settlers begin to join him.

1881

Phoenix is incorporated.

1906

Work begins on the Roosevelt Dam.

1912

Arizona becomes a state.

1930s

Phoenix becomes a tourist destination known for its exotic desert scenery.

Research

Unlike most of the country, Phoenix does not observe what seasonal change?

———

Spot the differences!

Can you find five differences between the two Sonoran Desert scenes below? You can color the landscapes, too!

The history of... Las Vegas

Nevada

Las Vegas

Time Line

1844
Explorer John C. Fremont sets up camp at present-day Las Vegas.

1858
Silver is discovered in Nevada.

1911
Las Vegas becomes an official city.

1931
Construction begins on the Hoover Dam. Gambling houses and saloons are built to entertain the workers, and gambling is soon legalized.

1950s
Land near Las Vegas is used by the government to test nuclear weapons.

Word Search!

Find the famous landmarks and people listed below. Words may be forward, backward, diagonal, or upside down.

```
V O F D C Z O O C A O H
O M U E S U M X A W K N
R P R E U V C T C G G U
C C A S I N O D T E C R
M N E A P U I M U L B G
X D R N G Q U G S I G B
H L C D T I A Z G S A A
O F H S R P T K A L T B
N L E T T E O P R A A T
R B H O O V E R D A M I
P Q U N D A N A E D A O
A O R E O L E P N R K C
```

Cactus Garden
Wax Museum
Hoover Dam
Sandstone
Casino

Research

The name "Las Vegas" is a Spanish phrase. What does it mean in English?

the meaDows

Dot-to-Dot!

Complete the dot-to-dot to draw the famous Las Vegas sign. You can even color it in!

The history of... *Seattle*

Washington

Seattle

Word Search!

Find the famous landmarks and features listed below.
Words may be forward, backward, diagonal, or upside down.

```
J C O F F E E S H O P S S
C I L W L N L Z L N O M P
A P M S U V C T E R G B A
N B X I V E H D T M C I C
A N E O H U I O A A B S E
L D P U G E T S O U N D E
S L C A T M N Z A D A A E
T F H J I P T D O I T Y E
C Z R X L R E L R S A N D
E B M O V P W E P I B E L
E I U A D A N A T A X B E
A T Z F N T I J O C E A N
E R A U Q S R E E N O I P
```

Puget Sound
Jimi Hendrix
Coffee Shops
Pioneer Square
Space Needle

Time Line

1850s

Settlers arrive in the Seattle area.

1889

A fire hits the city, and a new city is built on top of the ruins.

1896

Gold is discovered in nearby Canada and people begin settling in Washington.

1962

The Century 21 Exposition takes place, giving Seattle the Space Needle and the Monorail.

1979

Microsoft moves their headquarters to Seattle.

Research

How long has Seattle been home to humans?

———

Guide the bicycle through the park!

Seattle's mild climate allows for year-round outdoor activities, and bicycling is very popular. Can you lead this cyclist through the park to the coffee shop? Find the line that leads all the way through the park.

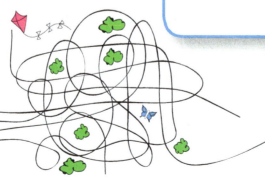

Start

End

The history of... *Los Angeles*

California

Los Angeles ★

Word Search!

Find the Los Angeles landmarks and features listed below. Words may be forward, backward, diagonal, or even upside down!

```
H O F D C Z O O O A O O
G E T T Y M U S E U M M
N P R S U V C T B G G D
E B X I V E D D O E C R
H O L L Y W O O D L B E
B D R A G Q D G A I G W
A L C A T R G Z A S A O
T F H J L P E K L L T T
E L E S T E R P I A A T
P B I O V P S E V N B I
A O U A D A N A A D A O
Y V E N I C E B E A C H
```

Hollywood
Getty Museum
Avila Adobe
Venice Beach
Dodgers

Time Line

1781
Spanish settlers arrive at El Pueblo de Los Angeles.

1876
A Central Pacific Railroad stop is established in Los Angeles, linking the city with the rest of the country.

late 1800s
Los Angeles' citrus industry grows, creating many jobs.

1910
The first film company is established in Los Angeles.

1913
The Los Angeles Aqueduct is completed, bringing water to the city.

1932
Los Angeles hosts the Summer Olympics.

Research

Dodger Stadium sells more of what than any other Major League baseball stadium?

_____

Make yourself a *star!*

The Hollywood Walk of Fame is filled with shiny pink stars with celebrities' names printed in gold. Want to be a star? Fill in your own name on the dotted line, then color your Walk of Fame star!

Great job!

_____

is an Education.com reading superstar

Learn the 50 States

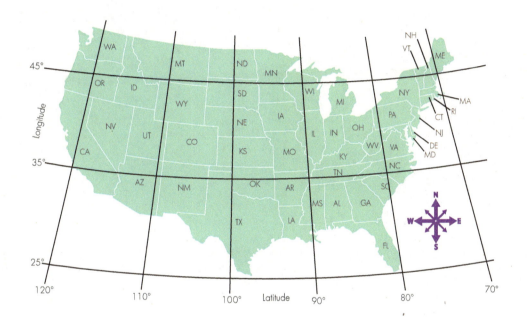

The United States of America

How well do you know you the states? Fill in the names of the states on the map below!

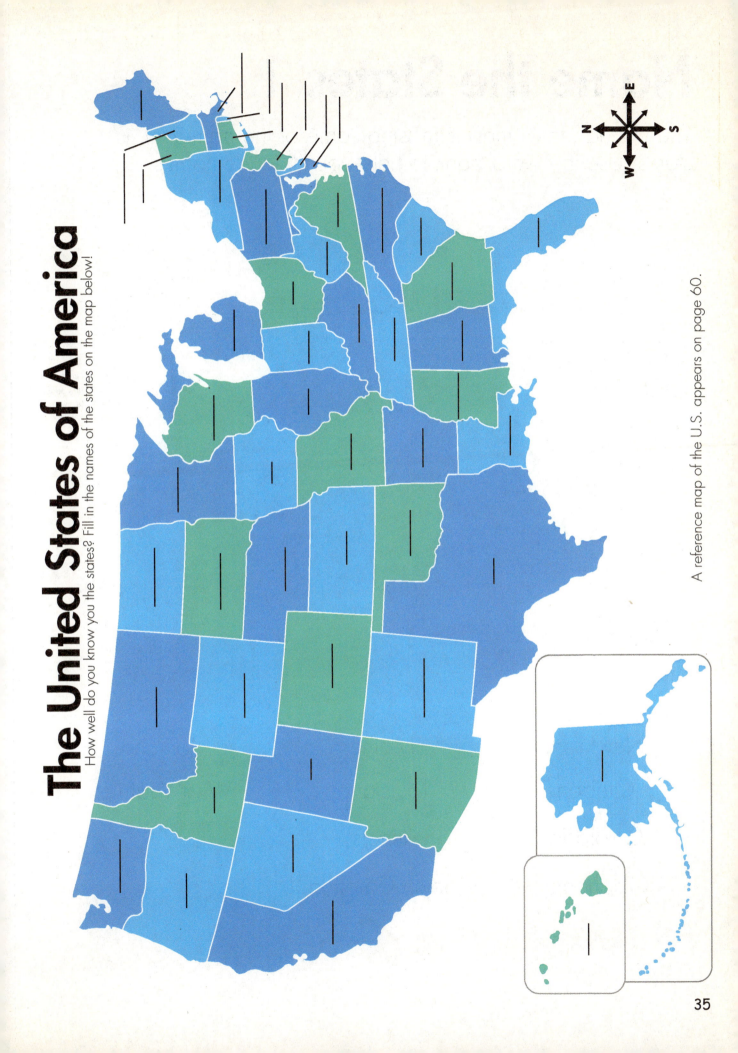

A reference map of the U.S. appears on page 60.

Name the States 1

The United States map is missing some of the names of its states! Use the word bank to help you fill in the names.

Note: Alaska and Hawaii are not to scale.

New York   Maine   Montana

Oregon   Louisiana   West Virginia

Colorado   Illinois

Oklahoma   South Carolina

Name the States 2

The United States map is missing some of the names of its states! Use the word bank to help you fill in the names.

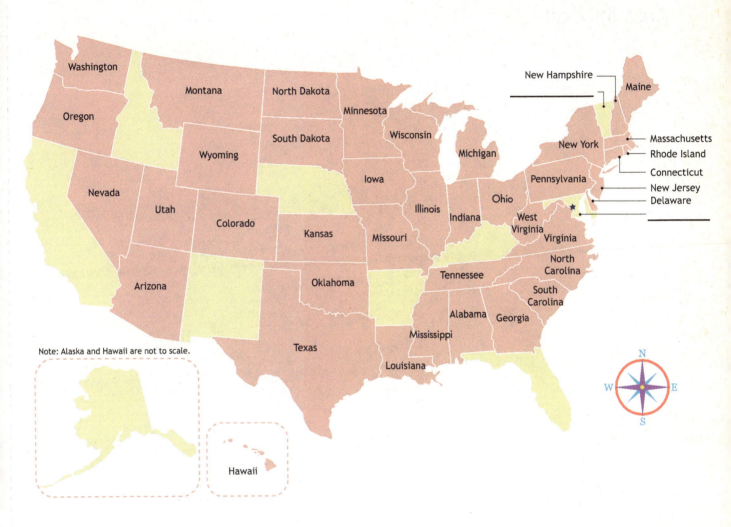

Note: Alaska and Hawaii are not to scale.

Idaho   Alaska   Nebraska

Florida   New Mexico   California

Arkansas   Kentucky

Maryland   Vermont

Road Trip!

Samantha and Jordan are going on a road trip from New York to California. They are going to stop at the capital of every state they pass through. Can you name the states they will pass through?

1 ⭐ _____

2 ⭐ _____

3 ⭐ _____

4 ⭐ _____

5 ⭐ _____

6 ⭐ _____

7 ⭐ _____

8 ⭐ _____

9 ⭐ _____

Food Road Trip Across The U.S.A!

Use your crayon to trace the route you would take to taste all the foods from around the country!

Color the States!

Color the state where you live red.
Color the states you have visited green.
Color the states you want to visit blue.

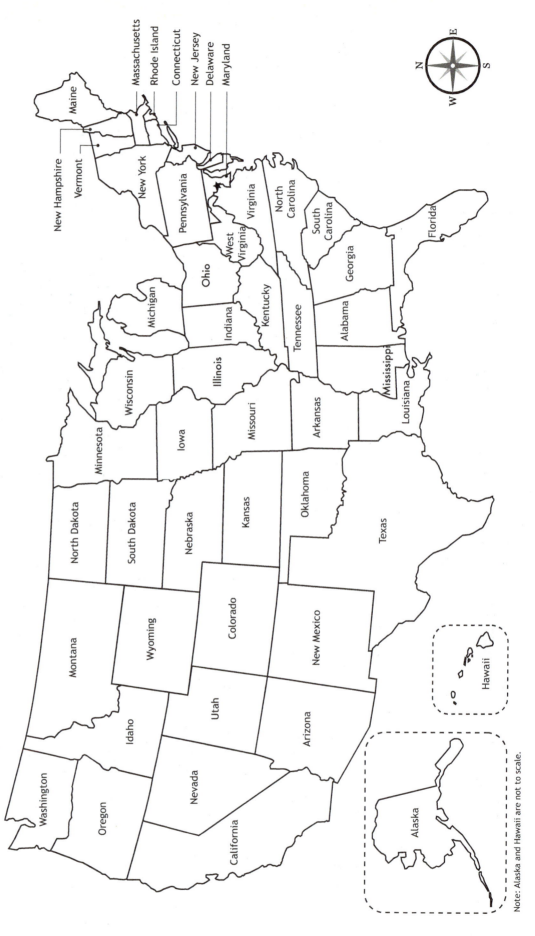

Note: Alaska and Hawaii are not to scale.

40

Color the States!

Look at the states you colored green. Why did you visit these states?

_____

_____

_____

_____

_____

_____

Look at the states you colored blue. Why do you want to visit these states?

_____

_____

_____

_____

_____

_____

What's That State? 1

Use a map to help you identify the states by their shapes.
You can also use the state capitals as clues.

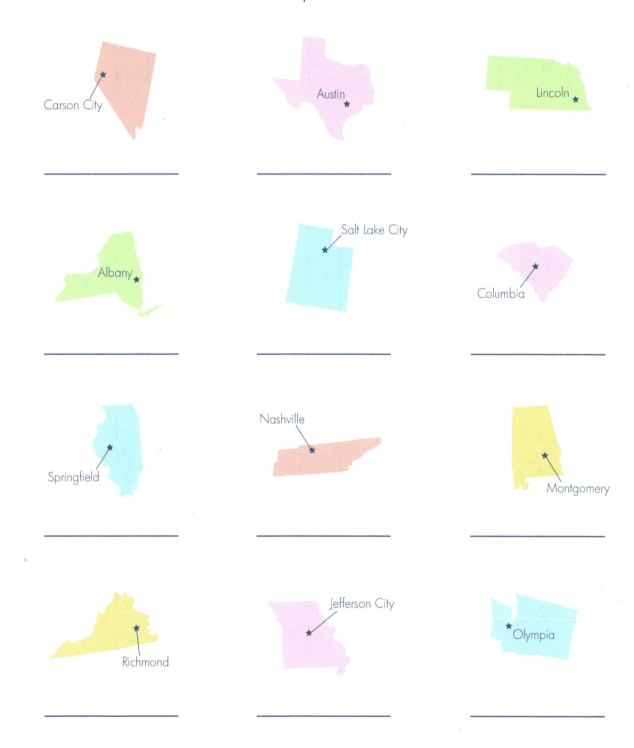

What's That State? 2

Use a map to help you identify the states by their shapes.
You can also use the state capitals as clues.

Make It Short!

Each state in the United States has its own two-letter postal abbreviation. Use the map on this page to find the postal abbreviation for every state.

Note: AK and HI are not to scale.

Alabama _____   California _____

Alaska _____   Colorado _____

Arizona _____   Connecticut _____

Arkansas _____   Delaware _____

Continue to write the postal abbreviation for every state.

Florida _____   New Jersey _____

Georgia _____   New Mexico _____

Hawaii _____   New York _____

Idaho _____   North Carolina _____

Illinois _____   North Dakota _____

Indiana _____   Ohio _____

Iowa _____   Oklahoma _____

Kansas _____   Oregon _____

Kentucky _____   Pennsylvania _____

Louisiana _____   Rhode Island _____

Maine _____   South Carolina _____

Maryland _____   South Dakota _____

Massachusetts _____   Tennessee _____

Michigan _____   Texas _____

Minnesota _____   Utah _____

Mississippi _____   Vermont _____

Missouri _____   Virginia _____

Montana _____   Washington _____

Nebraska _____   West Virginia _____

Nevada _____   Wisconsin _____

New Hampshire _____   Wyoming _____

Scrambled States!

Unscramble the names of the states below. If you need a hint, take a look at the picture bank!

1. THSOU KDAOTA	13. EWN EYEJSR
_ _ _ _ _ _ _ _ _ _	_ _ _ _ _ _ _ _ _
2. CMIHGAIN	14. SKASAN
_ _ _ _ _ _ _ _	_ _ _ _ _ _
3. YKNETKUC	15. LSINIOIL
_ _ _ _ _ _ _ _	_ _ _ _ _ _ _ _
4. AUTH	16. HAIDO
_ _ _ _	_ _ _ _ _
5. TEMOVRN	17. LDAFORI
_ _ _ _ _ _ _	_ _ _ _ _ _ _
6. GANIIVIR	18. WNE CMIXOE
_ _ _ _ _ _ _ _	_ _ _ _ _ _ _ _ _
7. SMIUSRIO	19. YADARNLM
_ _ _ _ _ _ _ _	_ _ _ _ _ _ _ _
8. GEONOR	20. GYMONIW
_ _ _ _ _ _	_ _ _ _ _ _ _
9. IMEAN	21. OEGGIAR
_ _ _ _ _	_ _ _ _ _ _ _
10. ABAALAM	22. SOAILIANU
_ _ _ _ _ _ _	_ _ _ _ _ _ _ _ _
11. CISSIWNON	23. TNCIOTCCEUN
_ _ _ _ _ _ _ _ _	_ _ _ _ _ _ _ _ _ _ _
12. HRNTO RALOACIN	24. HIOO
_ _ _ _ _ _ _ _ _ _ _ _	_ _ _ _
	25. DOOLACRO
	_ _ _ _ _ _ _ _

Picture Bank:

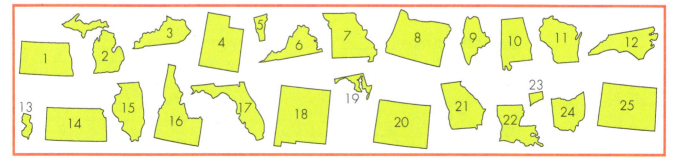

More Scrambled States!

Unscramble the names of the states below. If you need a hint, take a look at the picture bank!

26. NAMOANT _ _ _ _ _ _ _	38. DANVAE _ _ _ _ _ _
27. NWE PHIMAHSER _ _ _ _ _ _ _ _ _ _ _ _	39. SACASHETUSTMS _ _ _ _ _ _ _ _ _ _ _ _ _
28. HOAMOALK _ _ _ _ _ _ _ _	40. RNHOT KADOAT _ _ _ _ _ _ _ _ _ _
29. WAIO _ _ _ _	41. GOHIWANTSN _ _ _ _ _ _ _ _ _ _
30. DAIANIN _ _ _ _ _ _ _	42. RASKAANS _ _ _ _ _ _ _ _
31. RZAINOA _ _ _ _ _ _ _	43. YALNPNEVIANS _ _ _ _ _ _ _ _ _ _ _ _
32. HEDOR ALSIDN _ _ _ _ _ _ _ _ _ _	44. STEW NGIIVAIR _ _ _ _ _ _ _ _ _ _
33. NESTEESEN _ _ _ _ _ _ _ _ _	45. PSIPISIMSSI _ _ _ _ _ _ _ _ _ _ _
34. AXETS _ _ _ _ _	46. UTSHO OCRAILAN _ _ _ _ _ _ _ _ _ _ _ _
35. FLACOINARI _ _ _ _ _ _ _ _ _ _	47. WEAREALD _ _ _ _ _ _ _ _
36. EWN KYOR _ _ _ _ _ _ _	48. IHAIAW _ _ _ _ _ _
37. STMINEANO _ _ _ _ _ _ _ _ _	49. BANEKASR _ _ _ _ _ _ _ _
	50. KASAAL _ _ _ _ _ _

Picture Bank:

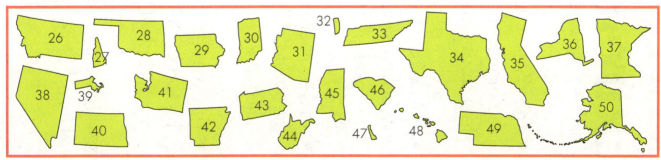

47

Extreme State Facts

Match each extreme fact to its state!

- The 49th state added to the United States also has the highest point in the U.S. (Mt. McKinley is 20,320 feet above sea level.)

- This western state has the largest salt lake in the western hemisphere. (The Great Salt Lake covers an average of 1700 square miles.)

- This southern state has the largest underground cave in the world. (The Mammoth - Flint cave system is 300 miles long.)

- This western state is home to the oldest living things in the world. (General Sherman, a 3500-year-old tree, and a stand of 4000-year-old bristlecone pines.)

- This western state has the smallest population in the United States.

Notable State Facts

Molly has collected her state facts, but can't remember which facts go with which states. Can you help her by drawing a line between the facts and their matching states?

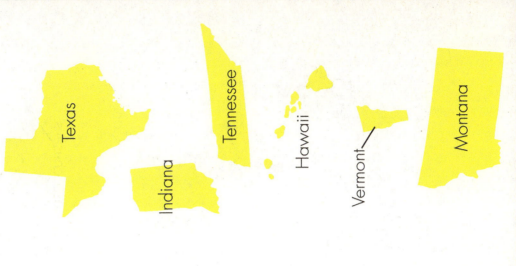

- This state is home to Grasshopper Glacier, named for the grasshoppers that can still be seen frozen in the ice.

- This state is the largest producer of maple syrup in the United States.

- Graceland, Elvis Presley's estate and burial site, is found in this state.

- This state is the site of the famous car race, the Indy 500.

- NASA is the headquarters for all piloted U.S. space projects and is found in this state.

- 'Iolani Palace, the only royal palace in the United States, is found in this state.

Going to the Coast

Match each fact with its east coast state!

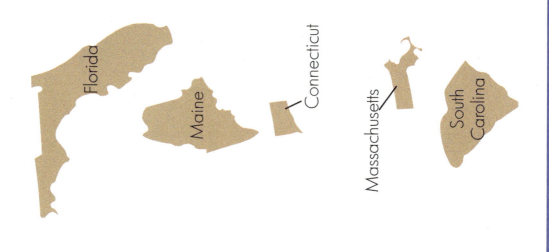

- The most easterly point in the United States, West Quoddy Head, is found in this state.

- This state is where the Boston Tea Party occured in 1773.

- The first battle of the Civil War took place at Fort Sumter in this state.

- Noah Webster, the author of the first dictionary, was born in this state in 1807.

- Known as the Venice of America, the city of Fort Lauderdale has 185 miles of local waterways and is found in this state.

Road Trip Across the USA

Tammy's family is taking a road trip! They want to visit the seven capital cities marked on the map. Draw a route for them to take and fill in the names of all the states they are going to pass through!

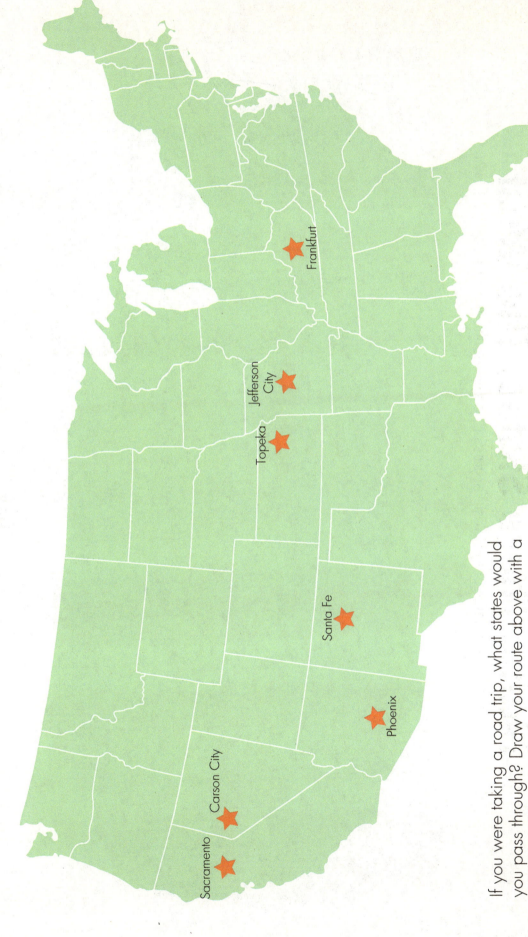

Frankfurt

Jefferson City

Topeka

Santa Fe

Phoenix

Carson City

Sacramento

If you were taking a road trip, what states would you pass through? Draw your route above with a different-colored pen.

Name These States: The West

Fill in the names of the western states to complete the map below!

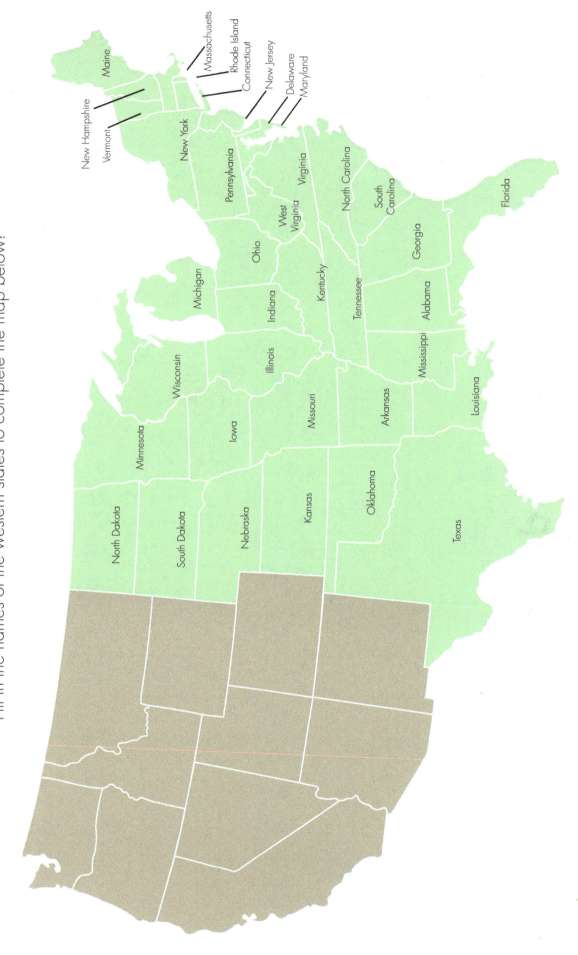

Name These States: The Midwest

Fill in the names of the mid-western states to complete the map below!

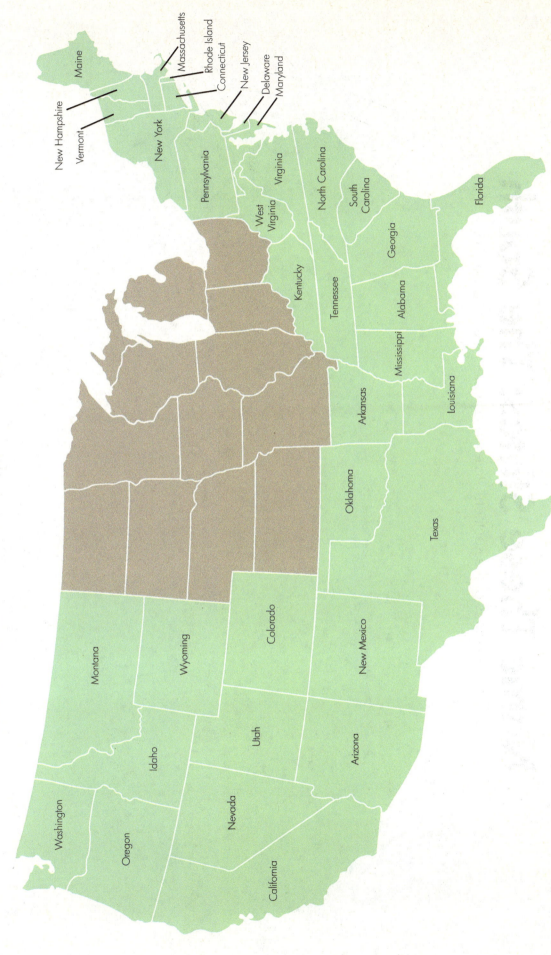

Maine

New Hampshire

Vermont

Massachusetts

Rhode Island

Connecticut

New Jersey

Delaware

Maryland

New York

Pennsylvania

West Virginia

Virginia

North Carolina

South Carolina

Florida

Kentucky

Tennessee

Georgia

Alabama

Mississippi

Arkansas

Louisiana

Oklahoma

Texas

Colorado

New Mexico

Montana

Wyoming

Idaho

Utah

Arizona

Washington

Oregon

Nevada

California

Name These States: The South

Fill in the names of the southern states to complete the map below!

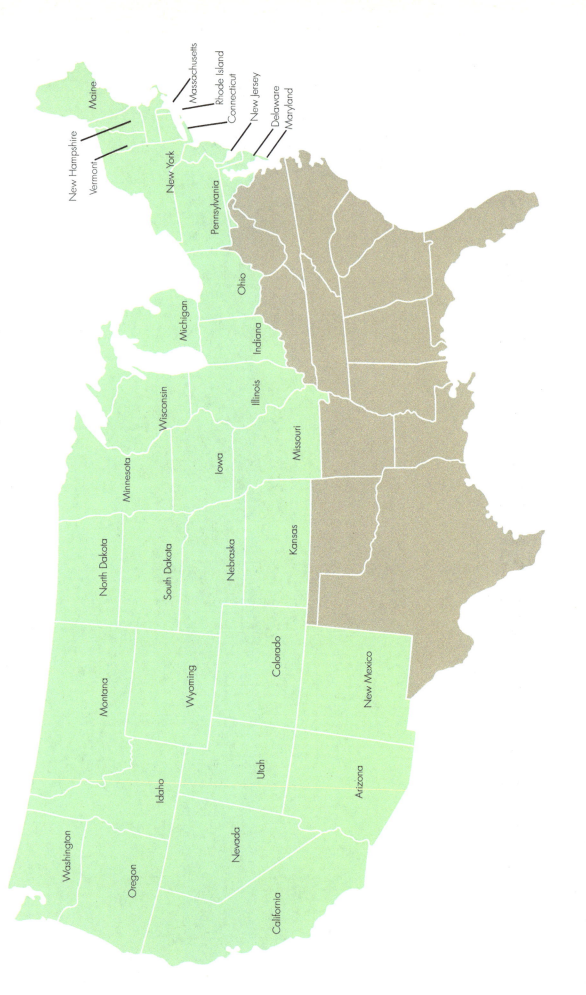

Name These States: The East Coast

Fill in the names of the East Coast states to complete the map below! The six states in orange form New England. **Note that some of the East Coast states are also southern states.**

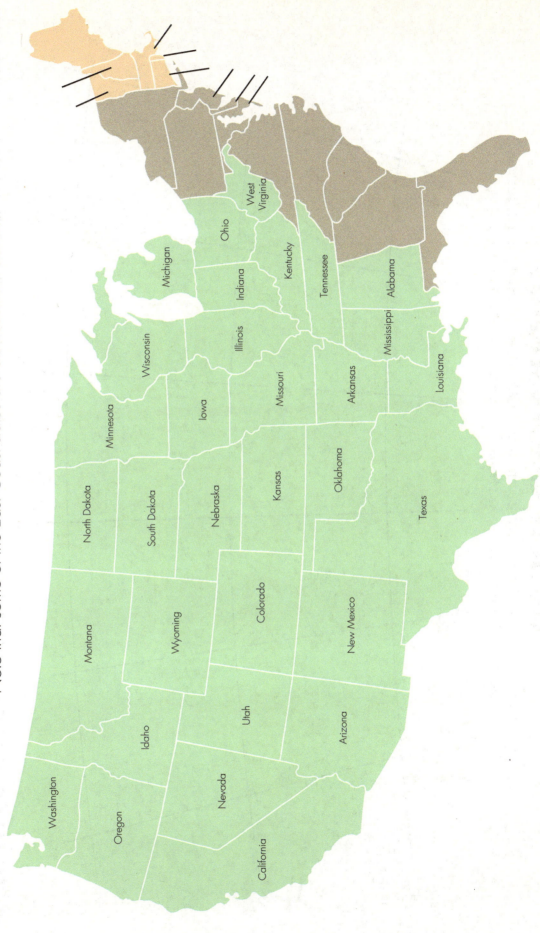

Launch Coordinates

Casey is looking for the perfect place to launch his rocket ship. He has found 4 possible locations. Use the coordinates below to locate the 4 states that Casey can launch from.

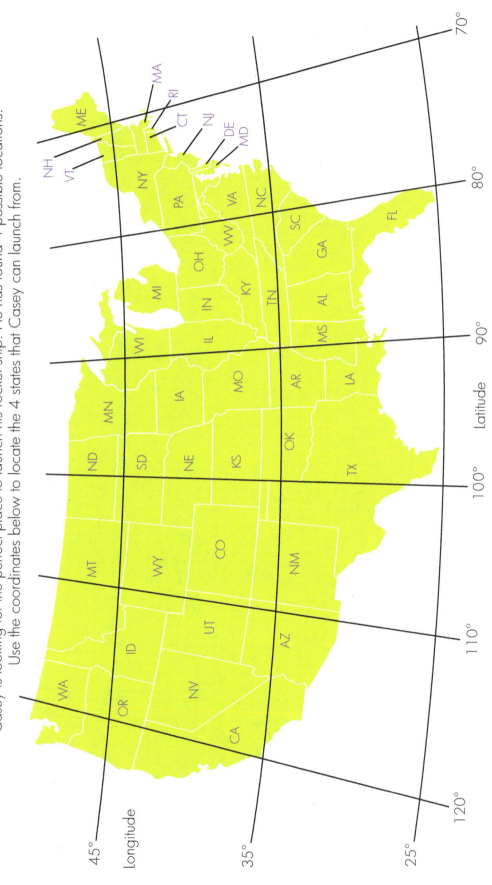

1. This location is at 30° north and 97° west: _____

2. This location is at 41° north and 78° west: _____

3. This location is at 39° north and 120° west: _____

4. This location is at 46° north and 108° west: _____

State Coordinates

Can you name the states located at the coordinates given below?

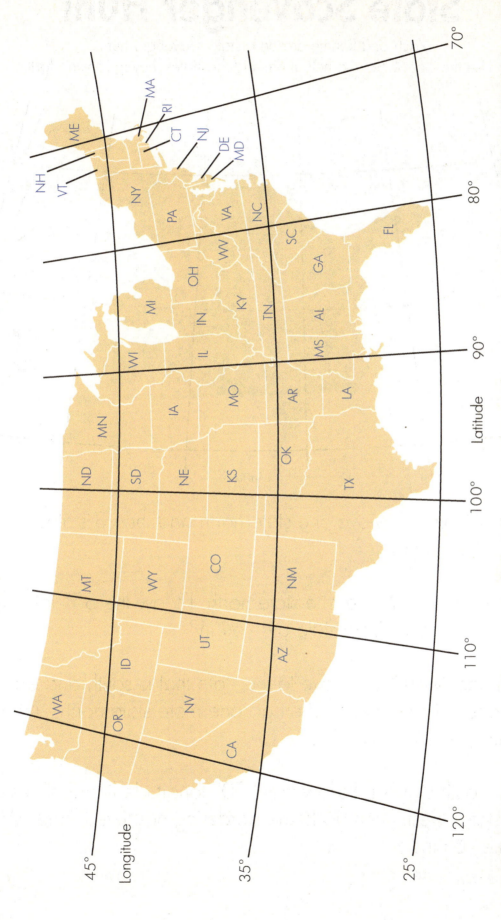

1. This location is at 37° north and 105° west: _____   2. This location is at 27° north and 82° west: _____

3. This location is at 44° north and 75° west: _____   4. This location is at 38° north and 91° west: _____

State Scavenger Hunt

Zach and Ronnie are on a state scavenger hunt.
Use the clues below to help them find the states they're looking for!

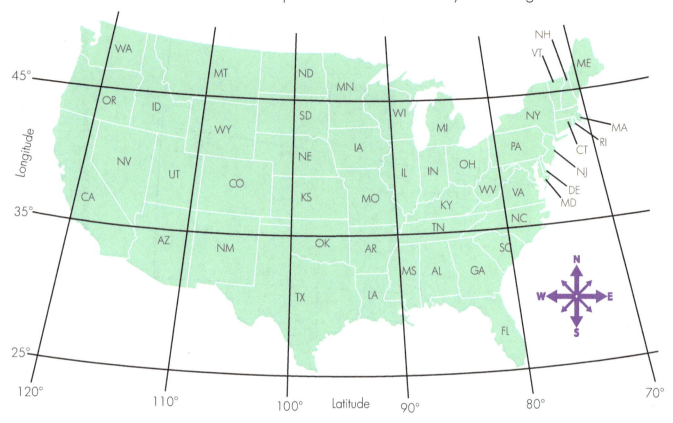

1. Start in Wyoming. Move one state north and then 3 states to the east. What state are you in?

2. Start in Alabama. Move one state north. Follow the 35° latitude line west 4 states. What state are you in?

3. Start in east Michigan. Move to the state that is south and east. Move one state northeast. Then go one more state north. What state are you in?

4. Start in South Dakota. Follow the 100° longitude line 2 states south. Go 2 states west. Then go to the bordering northwest state. What state are you in?

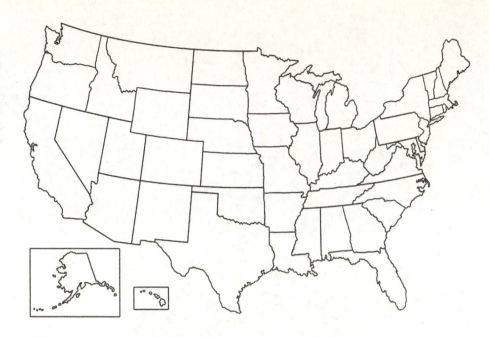

How many states can you name that start with these letters?

A _____

C _____

_____

D _____

F _____

G _____

H _____

I _____

_____

_____

_____

K _____

_____

L _____

M _____

_____

_____

_____

_____

_____

_____

_____

N _____

_____

_____

_____

O _____

_____

_____

P _____

R _____

S _____

_____

T _____

_____

U _____

V _____

_____

W _____

_____

_____

_____

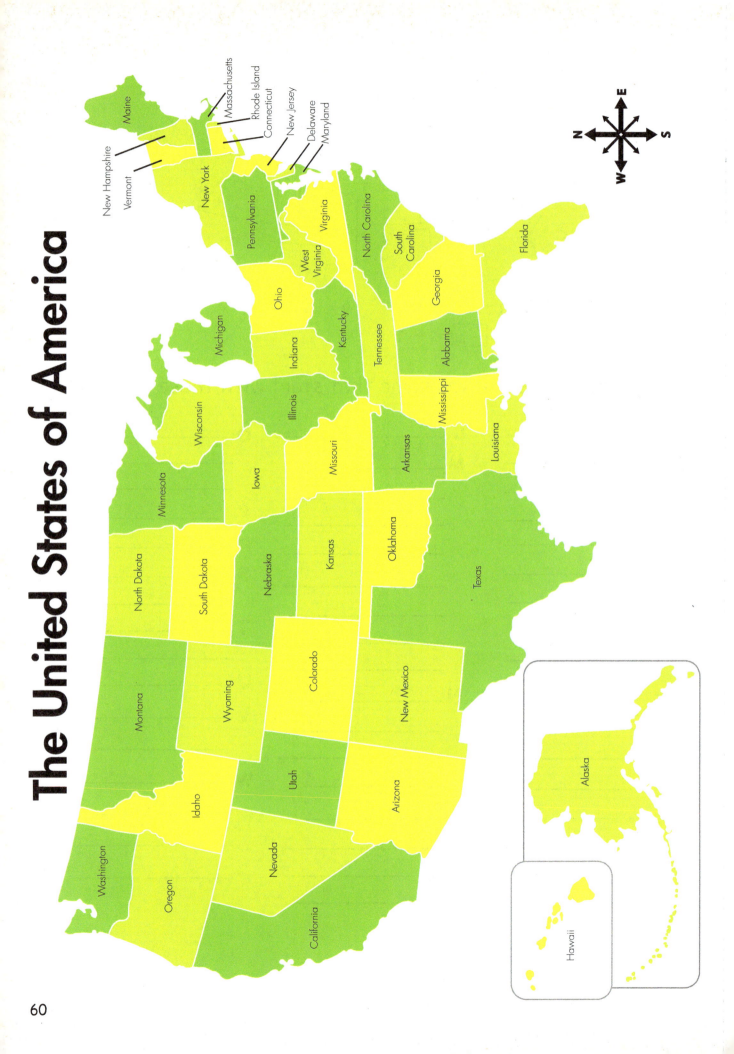

The United States of America

Great job!

is an Education.com social studies superstar

U.S. Capitals

Guess the Capital SCRAMBLE!

Get started by unscrambling the name of each state capital, then see if you can match it to its home state!

 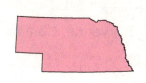 

NHEELA _____

JEUUNA _____

NNCLOLI _____

MNIROTPEEL _____

ORDNCCO _____

VDOER _____

UANSTI _____

XNHOEPI _____

ATSNA EF _____

BEIOS _____

ARHILEG _____

HCARNSTLEO _____

NEDSPRFILIG _____

ILLINOIS

ARIZONA

TEXAS

IDAHO

NEW MEXICO

NORTH CAROLINA

NEW HAMPSHIRE

NEBRASKA

MONTANA

ALASKA

DELAWARE

WEST VIRGINIA

VERMONT

Up, Down, and All Around!

See if you can name the missing state capitals using the capital cities of the states that surround them as clues.

For example:

<u>Salt Lake City</u>: Carson City, Boise, Cheyenne, Denver, Santa Fe, Phoenix

THIS CAPITAL	IS BORDERED BY
_____	: Topeka, Lincoln, Des Moines, Springfield, Frankfort, Nashville, Little Rock, Oklahoma City
_____	: Montpelier, Boston, Augusta
_____	: Santa Fe, Oklahoma City, Little Rock, Baton Rouge
_____	: Salem, Carson City, Phoenix
_____	: Montgomery, Atlanta
_____	: Indianapolis, Columbus
_____	: Trenton, Dover, Annapolis, Charleston, Columbus, Albany
_____	: Boise, Cheyenne , Bismarck, Pierre
_____	: Atlanta, Raleigh
_____	: Bismarck, Pierre, Des Moines, Madison

Go Fish... State Capitals Style!

Cut out these cards and use them to invent your own state capital quiz game!
Quiz yourself and your friends on state capitals and brush up on your U.S. geography skills as well. Look for some game ideas on the following pages to get you started!

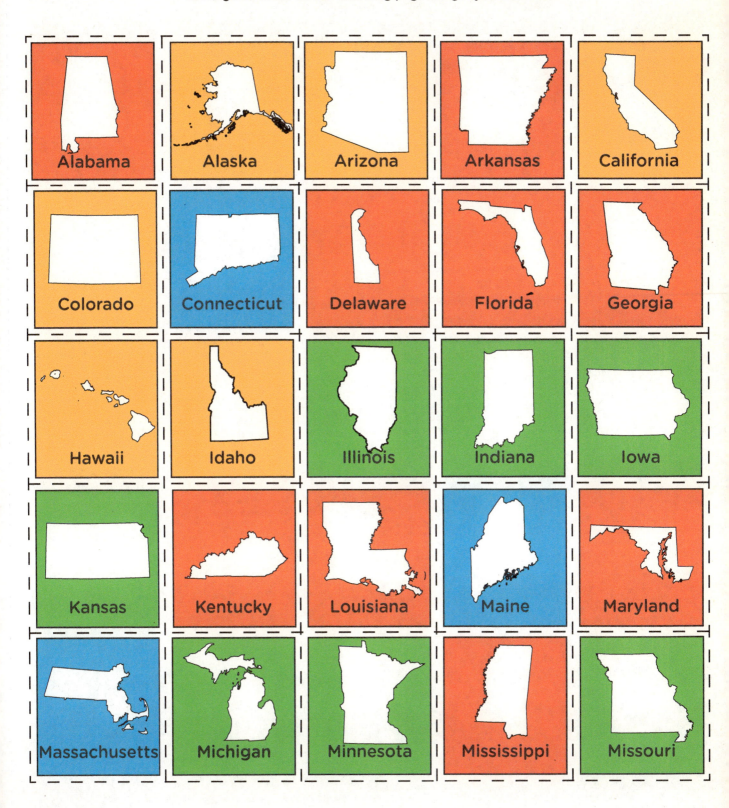

Alabama	Alaska	Arizona	Arkansas	California
Colorado	Connecticut	Delaware	Florida	Georgia
Hawaii	Idaho	Illinois	Indiana	Iowa
Kansas	Kentucky	Louisiana	Maine	Maryland
Massachusetts	Michigan	Minnesota	Mississippi	Missouri

Go Fish... State Capitals Style!

GAME IDEA: Give five cards to a friend and keep another five for yourself. Put the rest facedown in a pile. Instead of asking for numbers, ask for capital cities. For instance, challenge your friend by asking for 'the capital of Montana' instead of saying, 'Do you have Helena?' In order to win the game, you can either be the first to reach a certain number of cards, the first to gather all the states that start with A, or the first to gather all the cities in a certain area of the United States.

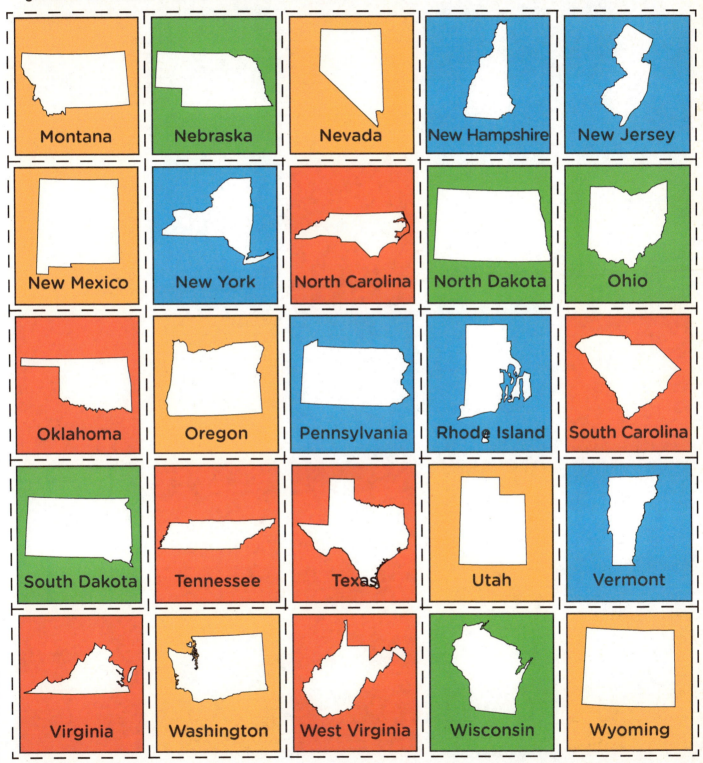

Montana	Nebraska	Nevada	New Hampshire	New Jersey
New Mexico	New York	North Carolina	North Dakota	Ohio
Oklahoma	Oregon	Pennsylvania	Rhode Island	South Carolina
South Dakota	Tennessee	Texas	Utah	Vermont
Virginia	Washington	West Virginia	Wisconsin	Wyoming

Go Fish... State Capitals Style!

GAME IDEA: Make two copies of the cards, then cut them out, and put them face down of the floor. Play a memory-match game to help memorize state shapes! These cards are endlessly flexible and are color-coded by region, so they'll work for a variety of activities.

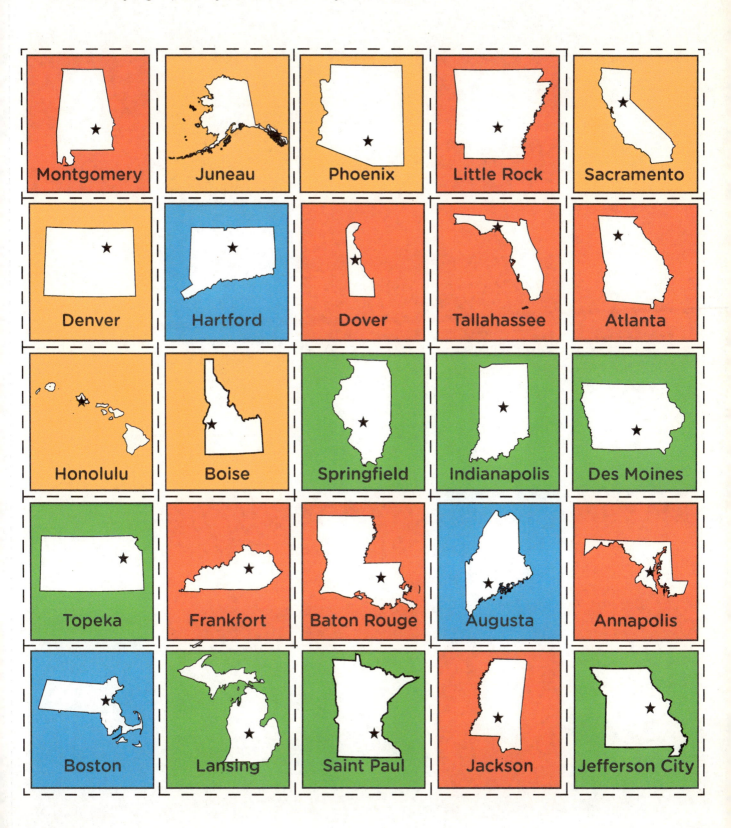

Montgomery | Juneau | Phoenix | Little Rock | Sacramento
Denver | Hartford | Dover | Tallahassee | Atlanta
Honolulu | Boise | Springfield | Indianapolis | Des Moines
Topeka | Frankfort | Baton Rouge | Augusta | Annapolis
Boston | Lansing | Saint Paul | Jackson | Jefferson City

Go Fish... State Capitals Style!

Regional color code key:

WEST · MIDWEST · NORTHEAST · SOUTH

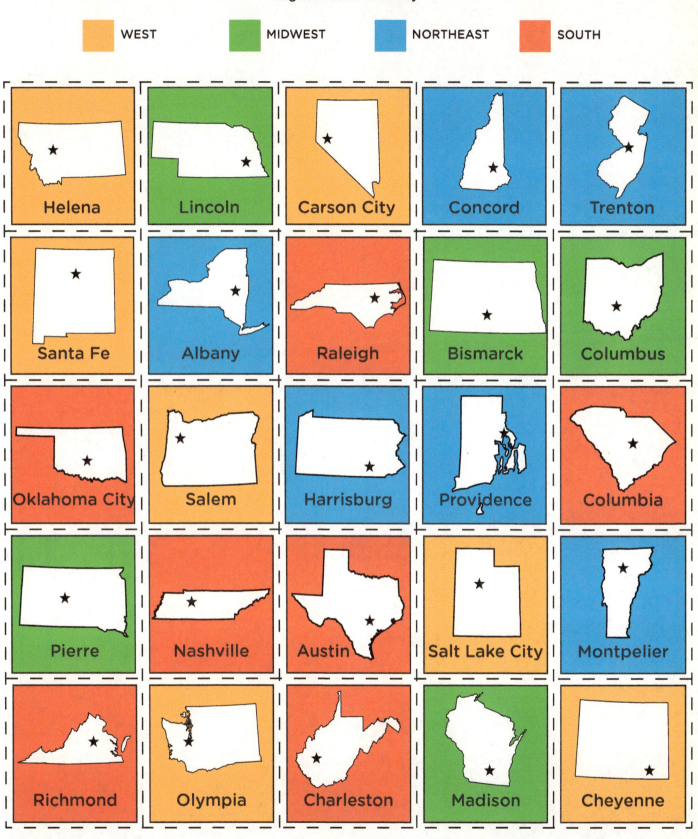

Helena	Lincoln	Carson City	Concord	Trenton
Santa Fe	Albany	Raleigh	Bismarck	Columbus
Oklahoma City	Salem	Harrisburg	Providence	Columbia
Pierre	Nashville	Austin	Salt Lake City	Montpelier
Richmond	Olympia	Charleston	Madison	Cheyenne

Alphabetical Order States

We've listed the number of states that start with a certain letter – see if you can name them all from memory! For more fun, print out a second copy and give one to a friend. Start a timer or a stopwatch and see who finishes first!

A

1. _____
2. _____
3. _____
4. _____

C

1. _____
2. _____
3. _____

D

1. _____

F

1. _____

G

1. _____

H

1. _____

I

1. _____
2. _____
3. _____
4. _____

K

1. _____
2. _____

L

1. _____

M

1. _____
2. _____
3. _____
4. _____
5. _____
6. _____
7. _____
8. _____

N

1. _____
2. _____
3. _____
4. _____
5. _____
6. _____
7. _____
8. _____

O

1. _____
2. _____
3. _____

P

1. _____

R

1. _____

S

1. _____
2. _____

T

1. _____
2. _____

U

1. _____

V

1. _____
2. _____

W

1. _____
2. _____
3. _____
4. _____

FROM   TO

75

That's MONUMENTAL!

Name the capital city by identifying the monument or Capitol building:

1. This city is known for its peaches and is home to the Coca-Cola headquarters.

2. This city was a hub for gold mining during the Gold Rush of 1849.

3. This state is home to "The Big Apple." What's the capital city?

4. This city sits just east of the Rocky Mountains.

5. This city played an important role in the American Revolution.

6. This city hosts a famous car race every year.

That's MONUMENTAL!

Name the capital city by indentifying the monument or Capitol building:

2. This city was a hub for gold mining during the Gold Rush of 1849.

Sacramento, California

1. This city is known for its peaches and is home to the Coca-Cola headquarters.

Atlanta, Georgia

4. This city sits just east of the Rocky Mountains.

Denver, Colorado

3. This state is home to "The Big Apple." What's the capital city?

Albany, New York

6. This city hosts a famous car race every year.

Indianapolis, Indiana

5. This city played an important role in the American Revolution.

Boston, Massachusetts

5 Facts: State Capitals Edition

Ever played 20 Questions? Here's a shortened version to help you memorize some state capitals!
Quiz your friends (or have them quiz you) with these trivia cards. See how fast you can name the capital!

5 Facts: State Capitals

- Singer Nat King Cole was born here, and Rosa Parks was born in nearby Tuskegee.
- I was the capital of the Confederacy during the Civil War.
- I was a major site during 20th-century Civil Rights movement.
- I'm in the central time zone.
- I'm the capital of Alabama.

5 Facts: State Capitals

- I'm home to many kinds of birds, bears, salmon and whales.
- My name is French.
- I'm the largest capital in area.
- I'm named after gold prospector Joe Juneau.
- I'm the capital of Alaska.

5 Facts: State Capitals

- I'm the 6th most populous city in the U.S.
- I'm larger in area than Los Angeles!
- I share a name with a mythical creature.
- I'm in the desert.
- I'm the capital of Arizona.

5 Facts: State Capitals

- I'm the home of the cheese dog!
- I was the site of a major event in the fight against school segregation.
- President Bill Clinton was born here.
- My name comes from a rock formation on the Arkansas River.
- I'm the capital of Arkansas.

5 Facts: State Capitals

- The Pony Express route used to end at here.
- I was the site of a major gold rush in the 1850s.
- I'm on the West Coast.
- I'm also called "Sactown" or "The River City."
- I'm the capital of California.

5 Facts: State Capitals

- I was the site of the Pike's Peak Gold Rush.
- I'm also called the "Mile-High City" because I'm one mile above sea level.
- I am just east of the Rocky Mountains.
- I'm named for Kansas Territory governor James W. Denver.
- I'm the capital of Colorado.

5 Facts: State Capitals

- Writer Mark Twain wrote some of his most famous books here.
- I'm in one of the original 13 colonies.
- I lie on the Connecticut River.
- I'm home to the oldest newspaper – The Hartford Courant.
- I'm the capital of Connecticut.

5 Facts: State Capitals

- I'm located on the St. Jones River.
- I was a stop on the Underground Railroad.
- I'm not in Pennsylvania, but I was founded by William Penn.
- I'm named for a city in England.
- I'm the capital of Delaware.

5 Facts: State Capitals Edition

Ever played 20 Questions? Here's a shortened version to help you memorize some state capitals!
Quiz your friends (or have them quiz you) with these trivia cards. See how fast you can name the capital!

Juneau, Alaska	Montgomery, Alabama
Little Rock, Arkansas	Phoenix, Arizona
Denver, Colorado	Sacramento, California
Dover, Delaware	Hartford, Connecticut

5 Facts: State Capitals Edition

Ever played 20 Questions? Here's a shortened version to help you memorize some state capitals!
Quiz your friends (or have them quiz you) with these trivia cards. See how fast you can name the capital!

5 Facts: State Capitals

- My name is from a Native American word for "old fields."
- I'm home to many colleges and universities.
- Like many other cities in my home state, I was settled by Spanish explorers.
- I'm located in the Florida Panhandle.
- I'm the capital of Florida.

5 Facts: State Capitals

- I hosted the 1996 Summer Olympics.
- I'm a large city, but I'm surrounded by forests.
- I'm known for my peaches.
- I'm in the South.
- I'm the capital of Georgia.

5 Facts: State Capitals

- I was part of a kingdom before my home state joined the union.
- President Obama was born here.
- Of all the cities in the U.S., I'm the furthest south.
- My home state is surrounded by water.
- I'm the capital of Hawaii.

5 Facts: State Capitals

- I'm sometimes considered to be part of the Pacific Northwest.
- I'm the capital of Idaho.
- I'm known for my potatoes.
- My nickname is the City of Trees.
- The inspiration for my name is from the French word for woods, "les bois."

5 Facts: State Capitals

- I am located in Sangamon County.
- My nickname is the Flower City.
- My name is the most common name for towns and cities in the United States!
- Abraham Lincoln moved to me in 1831, and lived here until he was elected.
- I'm the capital of Illinois.

5 Facts: State Capitals

- I'm in the Great Lakes region.
- I host a famous car race every year.
- I'm sometimes called "Indy" for short.
- My professional sports teams include the Colts and the Pacers.
- I'm the capital of Indiana.

5 Facts: State Capitals

- My downtown area is connected by skywalks.
- My name is French.
- I'm in the Midwest.
- I'm an important place for politics – the Iowa caucuses are held here during election years.
- I'm the capital of Iowa.

5 Facts: State Capitals

- I was founded in the 1800s as a free-state town, meaning slavery would not be legal there.
- I'm located in Tornado Alley, which means tornadoes occur frequently over me.
- My name means "to dig good potatoes" in Kansa.
- I'm on the Kansas River.
- I'm the capital of Kansas.

5 Facts: State Capitals Edition

Ever played 20 Questions? Here's a shortened version to help you memorize some state capitals!
Quiz your friends (or have them quiz you) with these trivia cards. See how fast you can name the capital!

Atlanta, Georgia	**Tallahasse, Florida**
Boise, Idaho	**Honolulu, Hawaii**
Indianapolis, Indiana	**Springfield, Illinois**
Topeka, Kansas	**Des Moines, Iowa**

5 Facts: State Capitals Edition

Ever played 20 Questions? Here's a shortened version to help you memorize some state capitals!
Quiz your friends (or have them quiz you) with these trivia cards. See how fast you can name the capital!

5 Facts: State Capitals

- I'm in the Southeast.
- The Kentucky River flows through me.
- I'm the fifth smallest state capital.
- I was named after pioneer Stephen Frank.
- I'm the capital of Kentucky.

5 Facts: State Capitals

- My name is French for "red stick."
- I'm known for my Cajun and Creole cultures.
- I'm the second-largest city in my state: the other is New Orleans.
- I'm located on the Mississippi River.
- I'm the capital of Louisiana.

5 Facts: State Capitals

- I'm located on the Kennebec River.
- I'm the easternmost state capital.
- I'm only 58 square miles large!
- I'm the capital of Maine.
- I am the third-smallest state capital.

5 Facts: State Capitals

- I was the temporary U.S. capital in 1783.
- I'm home to a famous Naval academy.
- I'm near Washington, D.C.
- I'm on the Chesapeake Bay.
- I'm the capital of Maryland.

5 Facts: State Capitals

- I was founded by the Puritans.
- I played an important role in the American Revolution.
- Some people call me "Beantown."
- I'm often considered the capital of New England.
- I'm the capital of Massachusetts.

5 Facts: State Capitals

- I am the only state capital that is not also a county seat.
- I'm in the Great Lakes region.
- My home state is shaped like a big mitten.
- I'm about 50 miles from Detroit.
- I'm the capital of Michigan.

5 Facts: State Capitals

- I'm on the east bank of the Mississippi River.
- I'm one half of the famous "Twin Cities."
- I'm on Central Standard Time.
- I'm named after one of the apostles in the Bible.
- I'm the capital of Minnesota.

5 Facts: State Capitals

- My nickname is "Crossroads of the South."
- I sit on top of an extinct volcano.
- I am famous for music like R&B, blues and gospel.
- I'm named for President Andrew Jackson.
- I'm the capital of Mississippi.

5 Facts: State Capitals Edition

Ever played 20 Questions? Here's a shortened version to help you memorize some state capitals!
Quiz your friends (or have them quiz you) with these trivia cards. See how fast you can name the capital!

Baton Rouge, Lousiana	**Frankfort, Kentucky**
Annapolis, Maryland	**Augusta, Maine**
Lansing, Michigan	**Boston, Massachusetts**
Jackson, Mississippi	**Saint Paul, Minnesota**

5 Facts: State Capitals Edition

Ever played 20 Questions? Here's a shortened version to help you memorize some state capitals!
Quiz your friends (or have them quiz you) with these trivia cards. See how fast you can name the capital!

5 Facts: State Capitals

- I'm on the northern edge of the Ozarks.
- I'm in the Midwest.
- I'm along the Missouri River.
- I'm named for President Thomas Jefferson.
- I'm the capital of Missouri.

5 Facts: State Capitals

- I was founded as a mining town.
- I'm close to the Continental Divide.
- I'm in the West.
- I'm in the shadow of the Rocky Mountains.
- I'm the capital of Montana.

5 Facts: State Capitals

- My nickname is the Star City.
- My name used to be Lancaster.
- I'm in the Midwest.
- I was named after our 16th president.
- I'm the capital of Nebraska.

5 Facts: State Capitals

- I was part of not a gold rush, but a silver rush, in the 1800s.
- I'm close to Lake Tahoe.
- I was a stopover for emigrants heading to California.
- I'm named after mountain man Kit Carson.
- I'm the capital of Nevada.

5 Facts: State Capitals

- My home state is one of the 13 colonies.
- I'm on Eastern Standard Time.
- I have a pretty small population – just over 40,000.
- The Middlesex Canal connects me with Boston, Massachusetts.
- I'm the capital of New Hampshire.

5 Facts: State Capitals

- I'm just across the river from Pennsylvania.
- I'm in the Delaware Valley.
- I'm right in the center of my state.
- I'm on Eastern Standard Time.
- I'm the capital of New Jersey.

5 Facts: State Capitals

- My name is Spanish.
- I'm in the Southwest.
- My nickname is "The City Different."
- I'm the capital of New Mexico.
- My full name used to be *La Villa Real de la Santa Fe de San Francisco de Asís*.

5 Facts: State Capitals

- I was founded as a Dutch trading post.
- I'm on the Hudson River.
- I'm about 150 miles north of a city called "The Big Apple."
- I'm named for the Duke of Albany.
- I'm the capital of New York.

5 Facts: State Capitals Edition

Ever played 20 Questions? Here's a shortened version to help you memorize some state capitals!
Quiz your friends (or have them quiz you) with these trivia cards. See how fast you can name the capital!

Helena, Montana	**Jefferson City, Missouri**
Carson City, Nevada	**Lincoln, Nebraska**
Trenton, New Jersey	**Concord, New Hampshire**
Albany, New York	**Santa Fe, New Mexico**

5 Facts: State Capitals Edition

Ever played 20 Questions? Here's a shortened version to help you memorize some state capitals!
Quiz your friends (or have them quiz you) with these trivia cards. See how fast you can name the capital!

5 Facts: State Capitals

- I'm known for my oak trees.
- The two closest cities to me are Durham and Chapel Hill.
- My home state touches the Atlantic Ocean.
- I'm named for explorer Sir Walter Raleigh.
- I'm the capital of North Carolina.

5 Facts: State Capitals

- I am on the east bank of the Missouri River.
- I am named after Otto von Bismarck.
- Lewis and Clark stopped by me near the beginning of their expedition.
- I was founded in 1872.
- I am the capital of North Dakota.

5 Facts: State Capitals

- I'm the largest city in my home state.
- I share a name with a famous explorer.
- My home state touches Lake Erie.
- I'm in the Eastern Time Zone.
- I'm the capital of Ohio.

5 Facts: State Capitals

- I grew quickly in the late 1800s thanks to the Homestead Act.
- My home state has a panhandle.
- I'm in the Great Plains region of the U.S.
- Put "City" after the name of my home state and you've got me!
- I'm the capital of Oklahoma.

5 Facts: State Capitals

- I am in the center of Willamette County.
- My nickname is the Cherry City.
- I share my name with a city in Massachusetts famous for their 17th-century witch trials.
- I am less than an hour's drive away from Portland.
- I'm the capital of Oregon.

5 Facts: State Capitals

- I'm in a region called the Rust Belt.
- I'm on the Susquehanna River.
- I played a big part in the Industrial Revolution.
- I'm known for my steel manufacturing.
- I'm the capital of Pennsylvania.

5 Facts: State Capitals

- I was founded by colonist Roger Williams.
- I'm located on Narragansett Bay.
- I'm one of the first established cities in America.
- The closest major city to me is Boston.
- I'm the capital of Rhode Island.

5 Facts: State Capitals

- I'm in two separate counties, Richland County and Lexington County.
- My name is also a poetic name used for the United States.
- My nickname is the Capital of Southern Hospitality.
- My state is on the East Coast.
- I'm the capital of South Carolina.

5 Facts: State Capitals Edition

Ever played 20 Questions? Here's a shortened version to help you memorize some state capitals!
Quiz your friends (or have them quiz you) with these trivia cards. See how fast you can name the capital!

Bismarck, North Dakota	**Raleigh, North Carolina**
Oklahoma City, Oklahoma	**Columbus, Ohio**
Harrisburg, Pennsylvania	**Salem, Oregon**
Columbia, South Carolina	**Providence, Rhode Island**

5 Facts: State Capitals Edition

Ever played 20 Questions? Here's a shortened version to help you memorize some state capitals!
Quiz your friends (or have them quiz you) with these trivia cards. See how fast you can name the capital!

5 Facts: State Capitals

- At only 13 square miles, I'm one of the smallest capital cities.
- I am on the Mississippi River.
- I am on Central Standard Time.
- I was named after a nearby fort.
- I'm the capital of South Dakota.

5 Facts: State Capitals

- I'm known for my country music scene.
- I'm located on the Cumberland River.
- My nickname is the Music City.
- My name was inspired by Fort Nashborough.
- I'm the capital of Tennessee.

5 Facts: State Capitals

- I'm known for my live music scene.
- I'm named for the Father of Texas, Stephen F. Austin.
- I am on the Colorado River.
- I am on Central Standard Time.
- I'm the capital of Texas.

5 Facts: State Capitals

- I was founded by Mormon settlers.
- I'm a popular spot for skiing.
- I'm in an area called the Great Basin.
- I'm located on a large lake.
- I'm the capital of Utah.

5 Facts: State Capitals

- I'm the smallest capital city.
- I'm named after a city in France.
- I'm near the Canadian border.
- I'm in New England.
- I'm the capital of Vermont.

5 Facts: State Capitals

- I am an independent city and not part of any county.
- My nickname is the River City.
- During the Civil War, I was the capital of the Confederate States of America.
- I am named after Richmond Hill in England.
- I'm the capital of Virginia.

5 Facts: State Capitals

- I'm on the Puget Sound.
- Some people call me "Oly" for short.
- I grew during westward expansion.
- Like the rest of my home state, I am known for my greenery.
- I'm the capital of Washington.

5 Facts: State Capitals

- I'm the largest city in my home state.
- I'm known for my coal mining industry.
- I'm in the Appalachian region.
- My home state was once part of Virginia.
- I'm the capital of West Virginia.

5 Facts: State Capitals Edition

Ever played 20 Questions? Here's a shortened version to help you memorize some state capitals!
Quiz your friends (or have them quiz you) with these trivia cards. See how fast you can name the capital!

Nashville, Tennessee	**Pierre, South Dakota**
Salt Lake City, Utah	**Austin, Texas**
Richmond, Virginia	**Montpelier, Vermont**
Charleston, West Virginia	**Olympia, Washington**

5 Facts: State Capitals Edition

Ever played 20 Questions? Here's a shortened version to help you memorize some state capitals!
Quiz your friends (or have them quiz you) with these trivia cards. See how fast you can name the capital!

5 Facts: State Capitals

- I am in the Midwest and Great Lakes regions.
- I am known for my popular college sports.
- I am often called the City of Four Lakes.
- I am named after President James Madison.
- I'm the capital of Wisconsin.

5 Facts: State Capitals

- I am on Crow Creek and Dry Creek.
- My nickname is the Magic City of the Plains.
- I was named after one of the Great Plains tribes.
- I am on the Mountain Time Zone.
- I'm the capital of Wyoming.

Review Your Cards

Use this space to keep track of the cards answered correctly and the cards that were answered incorrectly.
Arrange the cards and review the cards you are having trouble with. Can you move all cards to the green pile?

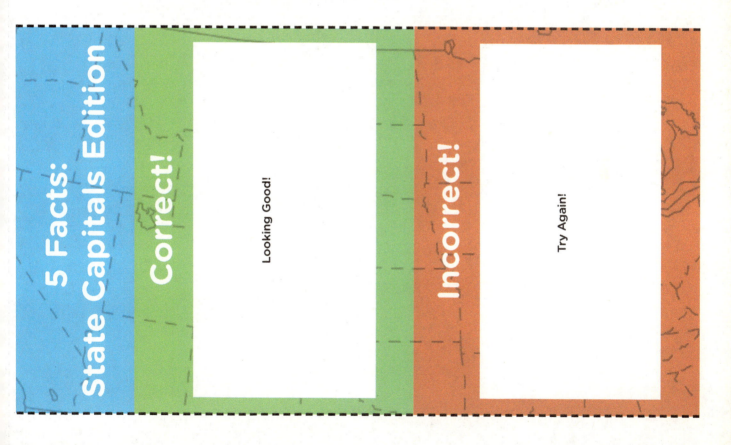

5 Facts: State Capitals Edition

Correct!

Looking Good!

Incorrect!

Try Again!

91

5 Facts: State Capitals Edition

Ever played 20 Questions? Here's a shortened version to help you memorize some state capitals!
Quiz your friends (or have them quiz you) with these trivia cards. See how fast you can name the capital!

Cheyenne, Wyoming

Madison, Wisconsin

Write a Rhyme

A great way to remember information is to make up a rhyme for it! Try to come up with a silly rhyming sentence for each state capital – we've added a few suggestions for each name to get you started. When you're done, recite them to your friends!

<u>EXAMPLE</u>

SACRAMENTO

Know, Go, Flow, So, Though, Row, Mow, Grow

You'll never know how far you can go 'til you visit Sacramento, California, where the palm trees grow!

SACRAMENTO

Know, Go, Flow, So, Though, Row, Mow, Grow

_____

_____

SALEM

Sail 'Em, Hem, Bail 'Em

_____

_____

OLYMPIA

The, Huh?

_____

_____

CARSON CITY

Pity, Gritty, Itty-Bitty

_____

_____

PHOENIX

Licks, Kicks, Nix, Nicks

_____

_____

SANTA FE:

Away, Day, Lay, Pray, Dismay

_____

_____

AUSTIN:

Lost In, Crossed In, Tossed In

_____

_____

OKLAHOMA CITY

Pity, Gritty, Itty-Bitty

_____

_____

DENVER

Tender, Render, Infer, Send Her

_____

_____

CHEYENNE

Shy Anne, Cry, Anne

_____

_____

JUNEAU

Y'know?

_____

_____

HONOLULU

You Do; You, Too

_____

_____

BOISE

Noisy

_____

_____

LINCOLN

Thinkin', Drinkin', Stinkin'

_____

_____

Write a Rhyme

BOSTON

Sun, Run, Son, Done, Ton

_____

_____

PROVIDENCE

Hence, Commence

_____

_____

DOVER

Over, Rover

_____

_____

ANNAPOLIS

Kiss, Miss

_____

_____

ALBANY

See, Tree, Knee, Agree

_____

_____

HARTFORD

Smart Bird, Art Nerd, Third, Blurred

_____

_____

HARRISBURG

How Absurd!

_____

_____

TOPEKA

Eureka!, Paprika

_____

_____

SALT LAKE CITY

Gritty, Itty-Bitty, Pity, Pretty

_____

_____

JACKSON

Action, Waxen, Flaxen

_____

_____

JEFFERSON CITY

Gritty, Itty-Bitty, Pity, Pretty

_____

_____

LITTLE ROCK

Shock, Crock, Lock, Jock, Knock

_____

_____

CHARLESTON

Charles' Ton, Carl's Done, Karl's Run

_____

_____

RICHMOND

Rich Blonde, Pond

_____

_____

AUGUSTA

Bust A, Just A

_____

_____

MONTPELIER

I Feel Ya

_____

_____

TALLAHASSEE

See, Free, Knee, Gee

_____

_____

PIERRE

Air, Lair, Care

_____

_____

Write a Rhyme

COLUMBIA

The, Huh? Duh

_____

_____

SPRINGFIELD

Heeled, Kneeled, Sealed

_____

_____

BATON ROUGE

Deluge, Subterfuge, Luge

_____

_____

INDIANAPOLIS

Happiness, Miss, This

_____

_____

COLUMBUS

Bus, Us, Rush

_____

_____

MONTGOMERY

See, Knee, Agree, Decree

_____

_____

HELENA

I'm Tellin' Ya

_____

_____

NASHVILLE

'Til, Still, Will, Drill

_____

_____

RALEIGH

See, Agree, Key

_____

_____

MADISON

Sun, Run, Fun

_____

_____

LANSING

Stand! Sing!, Can't sing

_____

_____

BISMARCK

His Mark, This Park, It's Dark

_____

_____

ATLANTA

The, Huh?

_____

_____

FRANKFORT

Report, Court, Tank Port

_____

_____

DES MOINES

Coin, Join, Purloin

_____

_____

ST. PAUL

All, Tall, Wall, Crawl, Gall, Drawl

_____

_____

TRENTON

Rent On, Vent On, Tent In

_____

_____

CONCORD

Word, Nerd, Herd

_____

_____

CRACK THE CODE

We've listed every state and its capital in alphabetical order by state. See if you can name all the states and their capitals using only the first letter of every word to help you!

A _____ : M _____

A _____ : J _____

A _____ : P _____

A _____ : L _____ R _____

C _____ : S _____

C _____ : D _____

C _____ : H _____

D _____ : D _____

F _____ : T _____

G _____ : A _____

H _____ : H _____

I _____ : B _____

I _____ : S _____

I _____ : I _____

I _____ : D _____ M _____

K _____ : T _____

K _____ : F _____

L _____ : B _____ R _____

M _____ : A _____

M _____ : A _____

M _____ : B _____

M _____ : L _____

M _____ : S ___.P _____

M _____ : J _____

M _____ : J _____ C _____

M _____ : H _____

CRACK THE CODE

We've listed every state and its capital in alphabetical order by state. See if you can name all the states and their capitals using only the first letter of every word to help you!

N _____ : L _____

N _____ : C _____ C _____

N ____ H _____ : C _____

N _____ J _____ : T _____

N ____ M _____ : S _____ F _____

N ____ Y _____ : A _____

N _____ C _____ : R _____

N _____ D _____ : B _____

O _____ : C _____

O _____ : O _____ C _____

O _____ : S _____

P _____ : H _____

R _____ I _____ : P _____

S _____ C _____ : C _____

S ____ D _____ : P _____

T _____ : N _____

T _____ : A _____

U _____ : S _____ L _____ C _____

V _____ : M _____

V _____ : R _____

W _____ : O _____

W _____ V _____ : C _____

W _____ : M _____

W _____ : C _____

State Capital Geo-Party!

Learn a little bit more about the state capitals in this quick round of contextual trivia.
Your trivia know-how won't be in jeopardy after this study session!

This capital is known as "Tally" to some locals.	This capital city is named after a large nearby lake. Some people might say it's "Great!"	This capital's name means "Red Stick" in French.
This capital was named for an American Indian nation.	This capital was home to a destructive "Tea Party" protest in 1773.	Rosa Parks refused to give up her seat on one of this city's buses, sparking a famous boycott.
This state's capital city was almost called Saint Peter!	This capital city was once claimed by Spain—not Mexico as you might think.	This is the capital of a state known mostly for its cheese production.
This capital is part of an island chain that is the most isolated population center on Earth.	This capital city is in a state that is two times the size of Texas.	This state capital produces many different crops—not just potatoes!

State Capital Geo-Party!

Learn a little bit more about the state capitals in this quick round of contextual trivia.
Your trivia know-how won't be in jeopardy after this study session!

Baton Rouge, Louisiana	**Salt Lake City, Utah**	**Tallahassee, Florida**
Montgomery, Alabama	**Boston, Massachusetts**	**Cheyenne, Wyoming**
Madison, Wisconsin	**Santa Fe, New Mexico**	**Saint Paul, Minnesota**
Boise, Idaho	**Juneau, Alaska**	**Honolulu, Hawaii**

Great job!

is an Education.com social studies superstar

Answers

Word Search *Answers*

Boston

```
F R N Z Y T I C Y D N I W
P A L W L N S Z L R O M X
O M N R I C A N U I Z E O
B A K E D B E A N S C I S
N N D O U E O A E B S D
M D I U Z I B X O R M D E
U L R A T M L Z A B A A R
S F B J I P G H O O T Y N
E Z R X L R S L A A A N O
U O E E I V C G E L O L T
M H W X N I I Z N S I B S
C H A R L E S R I V E R O
S C I T L E C N O T S O B
```

page 3

Washington, D.C.

```
S C A P I T O L H I L L Y
N I L W L N L Z L N O I P
U C I O D S T A S I E A H
P O T O M A C R I V E R C
X N E O H U T O A A B O E
I D P U Z E T X O U M R Q
N L C A T M N Z A T A T E
E F W H I T E H O U S E W
O Z R X L R E L R Z A M D
H O D E I V T F F K O L K
K E N N E D Y C E N T E R
A I Z F N O T J O N E A B
E R A U Q N R E E B O I P
```

page 4

Detroit

```
D E T R O I T T I G E R S
E S L W L N S Z L N O M P
T C L O D S R A S I E N H
R B X L V E A D T M C I C
O N E O U U E O A A B S E
I D P U Z B B X O U M G Q
T L C A T M O Z A T A N E
R F H J I P G G O A T I W
I Z R X L R A M O T O W N
V O D E I V C F E C O D K
E H O X N I I Z O N I E E
R T Z F N O H J O N E R B
L Q Z E Y T I C R O T O M
```

page 5

Chicago

```
S O N Z Y T I C Y D N I W
N S L W L N S Z L N O M P
K C L O D S R A S I E N H
R B X L V E A D T M C I C
A N E O U U E O A A B S E
P D P U Z B B X O U M D Q
N L C A T M O Z A T A A E
L F H J I P G G O A T Y W
O Z R X L R A L A Z A N D
C O D E I V C F E C O L K
N H O X N I I Z O N I B E
I T Z F N O H J O N E H B
L A K E M I C H I G A N C
```

page 6

104

Word Search *Answers*

Cleveland

```
B O N Z Y T I C Y D N I C
P R V I R I R U O S S I U
I C O O D S R A S I E N Y
S B X W V E A D T M C I A
H N E O N U E O A A B S H
M D P U Z S L H O U M D O
U L C A T M A I A T A A G
S F H J I P K A O A T B A
E Z R X L R E R R Z A O R
U O P E N G E I N M O T I
M H O X N I R V O N V Z V
R A Z I N D I A N S X Z E
C A V A L I E R S D G E R
```

page 7

Kansas City

```
I O N Z Y T I C Y D N I W
R E V I R I R U O S S I M
I C L O D S R A S I E N H
S B X L V E A D T M C I C
H N E O U U E O A A B S E
M D P U Z B R X O U M D Q
U L C A T M C Z A T A A E
S F H J I P H G O A T R W
E Z R X L R I L A Z A O D
U O D E I V E F E C O Y K
M H O X N I F Z O N I A E
J A Z Z F E S T I V A L B
Z A K V M I C B I G A S C
```

page 8

Miami

```
F O F D C Z O O O A G P M
C R L W L N L Z L N O M I
A P E S U V C T E R G B A
N B X N V E H D T M C I M
A N E O C U I O A A B S I
L D R A G H F G A R G C D
S L C A T M Q Z A D A A O
T F H J I P T U O I T Y L
C O R A L R E E F S A N P
E P M C V P W E P R E E H
E I U A D A N A T A T I I
A T L A N T I C O C E A N
J A F Z B U Z I C A Q Y S
```

page 9

Houston

```
H O U S T O N R O D E O S
O I L W L N L Z L N O M E
U P M S U V C T E R L B E
S B X I V E H D T E C I R
T N E O H U I O N A B S T
O D P U G Z T N O U N D A
N L C A T M A Z A D A A I
A F H J I H T D O I T Y L
S Z R X C R E L R S A N O
T B M P Y P W E P I B E N
R I I A D A N A T A X B G
C H Z F N T I J O C E A A
S P A C E C E N T E R A M
```

page 10

Word Search *Answers*

Albuquerque

```
H O T A I R B A L L O O N
R S L W L I S Z L X O L P
E M E R I O A N R I V D R
R B G L V G A D T Z C T C
T N D O U R E O A E B O E
A D I U Z A B X O R M W Q
E L R A T N N Z A U A N E
H F B J I D C W O O T Y W
T Z R X Z E N A O A A N D
O O E F I V C G F T O L K
M H W E S T M E S A D B E
I T O F N O H J O I E L B
K X T E M I C B I G K N O
```

Portland

```
J C O F Z X F B H O R S S
C O L U M B I A R I V E R
A P R S U V C T E R G B E
N B X E V E H D T M R I Z
A N E O G U I O A A E S A
L D P U G O T S O U E D L
S L C A T M N Z A D N A B
T F H J I P T Z O I C Y L
C O R A L R E E O S I N I A
E B M O V P W E P O T E A
E I U A D A N A T A Y B R
A T Z E N T I J O C E A T
E S K O O B S L L E W O P
```

San Francisco

```
H O F D C Z O O O O A O O
G Q L W L N L Z L N K M
N P R S U V C T E G G D
E B X I V E H D R E C R
M N E O P U I V A L B E
B D R A G O N G A I G W
A L C A T R A Z A S A O
T F H J L P I K O L T O
E L E S T F O R T A A T
P B I O V P W E R N B I
A O U A D A N A T D A O
Y T R G E G W G O S N C
```

Honolulu

```
D O F D C Z O U O A O G
G I T T Y M U N E U M A
N P A S U V C I D G G Y
S M A M S I U O L T S A
H O Z D O N A C L O V B
B D R A G N D S A I G A
X L C X O R D T A S A M
T F H W L P E H L L T U
S U G A R C A N E A A
P B I S L A N I D A A N
A O U A D A N O A D D A
W A I K I K I B E A C H
```

Word Search *Answers*

New York City

```
S R N Z Y Z I C Y S N I N
L T L W L N S Z L C O M E
V M O R I C A N R E V E W
I B C C R E A D T N C I A
S N D O K E O A T B S M M
P D I U Z E V X O R M D S
R L R A T M X E A A A A T
E F B J I P G C F L T Y E
S Z R X Y D N A H P W N R
L O E B R O A D W A Y L D
E H W X N I I Z N R N T A
Y T O F N O H J O K E G M
L X T I M E S S Q U A R E
```

page 15

Pittsburgh

```
P O N Z Y T I C Y D N I W
R I V I R I R U O S S I M
I C R O D S R A S I E N H
S B X A V E A D T M C I C
H N E O T U E O A A B S E
M D P U Z E R B H O U M D S
U L C A T M S I A T A A R
S F H J I P H O D A T B E
E Z R X L R I R A Z A O L
U O P E N G U I N S O T E
M H O X N I F V O N I Z E
R A Z T F F B F I V X L T
C I T Y O F B R I D G E S
```

page 19

Minneapolis

```
T W I N S V I C H I L L Y
U I L W L N L Z L N O C P
N E M A D S T A S I E I H
I X T B B A C R I V E T C
O T E O E A I O A A B Y E
N E P U Z R M X O U M O Q
S R C A T M W A A T A F E
T A W H R I V O P W A L K
A V R X L R E L L I A A D
T E D E Y V T F F V V K K
V I K I N G S R E T E F D
O U Z F X O I J O N E S R
N E A U Q N R E E B O I P
```

page 20

Baltimore

```
F O F D C Z O O O O A O H
O Q L W L N L Z L N K T
R P R E U V C T E G G U
T B X S V E H D R E C R
M N E U P U I M A L B E
C D R O G Q U G A I G B
H L C H T I A Z A S A A
E F H G R P T K O L T B
N L E A T E O P T A A T
R B U L V P W E P N B I
Y Q U F D A N A T D A O
A O R I O L E P A R K C
```

page 21

107

Word Search *Answers*

St. Louis

```
H O F D C Z O U O A O G
G E T T Y M U N E U M A
N P R S U V C I D G G T
S M A R S I U O L T S E
H O Z D Y W G N D L B W
B D R A C T D S A I G A
X L C X O R G T A S A Y
T F H W L P E A L L T A
E L N S T E R T I A A R
P B I S L A N I D R A C
A O U A D A N O A D A H
Y V E N I C E N E A C H
```

page 22

New Orleans

```
F O F D C Z O O O A O O F
C R L W L N L Z L N K M G
A P E S U V C T E G G D N
N B X N V E H D R M C R A
A N E C C I V A A B E Y
L D R A C H N G A R G W A
S L C A T R Q Z A D A O L
T F H J L P T U O I T T A
R L R Z S B A N A G A T B
E B I O V P W E F R B I M
E O U A D A N A T A T O A
T T R G E G W G Q S N E J
J A Z Z M U S I C A O O R
```

page 23

Montgomery

```
R A W L I V I C H I L L Y
U D L W L N L Z L N O I P
N E A A D S T A S I E A H
I X T G B A C R I V E R C
O T E O A A I O A A B O E
N E P U Z O M X O U M R Q
S R C A T M A A A T A T E
T A W H R I V E R W A L K
A V R X L R E L Y I A M D
T E D E I V T F E N V L K
I N N E D Y R E T X E D
O U Z F N O I J O N E R R
N E A U Q N R E E B O I P
```

page 24

Nashville

```
R A D N O R L A K E O F C
X I L W C N O Z G N O R O
A O M S I C N A R O G A U
H S Z N S N C B A X F N N
A N E N U C I S N A S C T
L D P U T E N S D U O I R
S L C A T R B Z O D K S Y
T F H J I P O D L I C N M
C Z R X L R W M E S I A U
E B M O V P L E O I H S S
S R E G N A R S P S D H I
A T Z E N T I J R C I A C
M U S I C C I T Y N O P T
```

page 25

Word Search *Answers*

Phoenix

```
S O N O R A N D E S E R T
N I L W L N L Z L N O M P
U N I O N S T A T I O N H
S B X I V E H D T M C I C
X N E O H U I O A A B S E
I D P U Z E T X O U M D Q
N L C A T M N Z A T A A E
E F H J I P T D O A T Y W
O Z R X L R E L R Z A N D
H O L E I N T H E R O C K
P H O E N I X Z O O X B E
A I Z F N O I J O N E A B
E R A U Q N R E E B O I P
```

page 26

Las Vegas

```
F O F D C Z O O C A O H
C M U E S U M X A W K T
R P R E U V C T C G G U
T C A S I N O D T E C R
M N E A P U I M U L B E
C D R N G Q U G S I G B
H L C D T I A Z G S A A
E F H S R P T K A L T B
N L E T T E O P R A A T
R E H O O V E R D A M I
Y Q U N D A N A E D A O
A O R E O L E P N R K C
```

page 27

Seattle

```
J C O F F E E S H O P S S
C I L W L N L Z L N O M P
A P M S U V C T E R G B A
N B X I V E H D T M C I C
A N E O H U I O A A B S E
L D P U G E T S O U N D E
S L C A T M N Z A D A A E
T F H J I P T D O I T Y E
C Z R X L R E L R S A N D
E B M O V P W E P I B E L
E I U A D A N A T A X B E
A T Z E N T I J O C F A N
E R A U Q S R E E N O I P
```

page 28

Los Angeles

```
H O F D C Z O O G A O O
G E T T Y M U S E U M M
N P R S U V C T B G G D
E B X I V E D D O E C R
H O L L Y W O O D L B E
B D R A G Q D G A I G W
A L C A T R G Z A S A O
T F H J L P E K L L T T
E L E S T E R P I A A T
P B I O V P S E V N B I
A O U A D A N A A D A O
Y V E N I C E B E A C H
```

page 29

109

Quiz and Activity *Answers*

Boston page 3

Quiz

Q: Boston Harbor has 34 _____ .

A: Islands. Together, the 34 islands form Boston Harbor Islands National Park Area.

Activity

1. To get from Forest Hills station to Oak Grove station, take the _____ORANGE_____ Line.
2. To get from Lechmere station to Heath station, take the _____GREEN_____ Line.
3. To get from Alewife station to Mattapan station, take the Red Line and transfer at ___ASHMONT___ station.

Washington, D.C. page 4

Quiz

Q: How is Washington, D.C. different from all other U.S. states?

A: It has no Congressional representative. Washington, D.C. is what's called a "federal district," not an official state.

Activity

A: The Washington Monument, built in 1884 to honor first U.S. President George Washington.

Detroit page 5

Quiz

Q: Detroit is the _____ city in the state of Michigan.

A: Largest. Detroit has a population of over 700,000 people!

Activity

1) Star hood ornament on #1. 2) Bumper on #1 is bigger. 3) No round headlights on #1. 4) Top lights on #1 are closer together. 5) #2 has windshield wipers.

Chicago page 6

Quiz

Q: How did Chicago get its name?

A: The most likely explanation is that "Chicago" comes from the word *shikaakwa*, meaning "wild onion" in Algonquin, a Native American language.

Activity

1) C - Lake Michigan, 2) E - Lake Erie, 3) B - Lake Huron, 4) D - Lake Ontario, 5) A - Lake Superior

Cleveland page 7

Quiz

Q: Cleveland's first resident was a settler named _____ .

A: Lorenzo Carter. He built a two-room log cabin on the banks of the Cuyahoga River.

Activity

1) Bridge (at bottom of strings) missing.
2) Bell-shaped decoration at top missing.
3) Control dial missing. 4) Tuning pegs missing. 5) No strap peg (on top right curve).

Kansas City page 8

Quiz

Q: Kansas City has the second-highest number of _____ of any city in the world.

A: Fountains. Only Rome, Italy has more. One of Kansas City's nicknames is the City of Fountains.

Activity

A: Five instruments. Trumpet, trombone, clarinet, bass, saxophone.

Quiz and Activity *Answers*

Miami page 9

Quiz

Q: Fill in the blank: Miami is the only city in the United States to lie between two _____.

A: National parks. Miami lies between Everglades National Park and Biscayne National Park.

Activity

A: There are 10 starfish.

Houston page 10

Quiz

Q: Houston is different from all other Texas cities in what way?

A: It is the largest city in Texas. It also has the fourth-largest population in the United States.

Activity

1) MISSION CONTROL, 2) SPACE STATION

Albuquerque page 11

Quiz

Q: The word "KiMo" means "mountain lion" in what language?

A: Tewa, a Native American language spoken by the Pueblo peoples.

Activity

1) D - A hand, 2) C - Yucca pod, 3) B - Unknown bird, 4) A - Macaw bird

Portland page 12

Quiz

Q: Portland is also known by what flower-related nickname?

A: City of Roses. Roses thrive in Portland's climate. It is home to the annual Portland Rose Festival.

Activity

1) Matt Groening, 2) Twilight, 3) Beverly Cleary

San Francisco page 13

Quiz

Q: What dessert is reported to have been invented at the Japanese Tea Garden in San Francisco?

A: Fortune cookies

Honolulu page 14

Quiz

Q: What does the Hawaiian word "honolulu" mean?

A: "Sheltered bay" or "place of shelter"

Activity

1) C - Plumeria, 2) B - Bird of Paradise, 3) A - Hibiscus

Quiz and Activity *Answers*

New York City **page 18**

Quiz

Q: What island, located in New York Bay, belongs in part to New York City and in part to Jersey City, New Jersey?

A: Ellis Island. Located in the Upper Bay, it was the nation's busiest immigration station between 1892 and 1954.

Activity

1) E - Bronx, 2) A - Manhattan, 3) C - Queens, 4) B - Brooklyn, 5) D - Staten Island

Minneapolis **page 20**

Quiz

Q: The name "Minneapolis" combines words from what two languages?

A: Greek and Dakota, a Native American language. It is a combination of Greek *polis*, meaning city, and Dakota *mni*, meaning water.

Activity

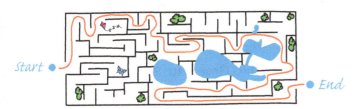

St. Louis **page 22**

Quiz

Q: The St. Louis area is home to a park, animal farm, and historical site named for what U.S. President?

A: Ulysses S. Grant

Activity

1) Bird furthest to right is different. 2) Top right leaves are different. 3) Extra limb on second tree. 4) Extra shrub beside first tree. 5) Leaf falling from tree.

Pittsburgh **page 19**

Quiz

Q: Pittsburgh lies at the meeting point of the _____ and _____ Rivers.

A: Allegheny and Monongahela. Pittsburgh's central business district lies at the confluence, or meeting place, of the two rivers.

Activity

1) B - 10th Street Bridge, 2) C - Smithfield Street Bridge, 3) A - California Avenue Bridge

Baltimore **page 21**

Quiz

Q: What kind of craft was successfully launched in Baltimore for the first time in U.S. history?

A: An air balloon

Activity

1) Mane on #2 is shorter. 2) Tail on #2 is moving. 3) Spot on hoof of #1. 4) Front legs on #1 are closer together. 5) Extra spot on #2.

New Orleans **page 23**

Quiz

Q: What did the French originally name New Orleans, and what did the name mean?

A: La Nouvelle-Orléans, meaning "The New Orléans." It was called "new" because France already had a city by that name.

Quiz and Activity *Answers*

Montgomery page 24

Quiz

Q: Montgomery was the first U.S. city to have a city-wide _____ system.

A: Electric streetcars. It replaced a system of horse-drawn streetcars.

Activity

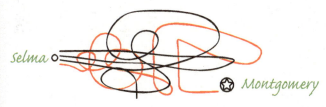

Selma ○

⬠ Montgomery

Nashville page 25

Quiz

Q: A copy of the ancient Greek structure, the _____, stands in Nashville's Centennial Park.

A: Parthenon. The original Parthenon was completed in Athens, Greece in 438 B.C.

Activity

1) C - Pedal Steel Guitar, 2) A - Dobro, 3) B - Zither

Phoenix page 26

Quiz

Q: Unlike most of the country, Phoenix does not observe what seasonal change?

A: Daylight Saving Time, when people temporarily turn their clocks forward so afternoons have more daylight hours.

Activity

1) Cactus in #2 is gone. 2) Extra cloud in sky in #2. 3) Rock in #1 is smaller. 4) Fewer mountains in #2. 5) Fewer spots on gila monster in #2.

Las Vegas page 27

Quiz

Q: The name "Las Vegas" is a Spanish phrase. What does it mean in English?

A: The meadows

Seattle page 28

Quiz

Q: How long has Seattle been home to humans?

A: Over 4,000 years! Most of that time, Native Americans were the main residents. European settlers arrived in the 19th century.

Activity

Start

● End

Los Angeles page 29

Quiz

Q: Dodger Stadium sells more of what than any other Major League baseball stadium?

A: Hot dogs

Name the States 1

The United States map is missing some of the names of its states! Use the word bank to help you fill in the names.

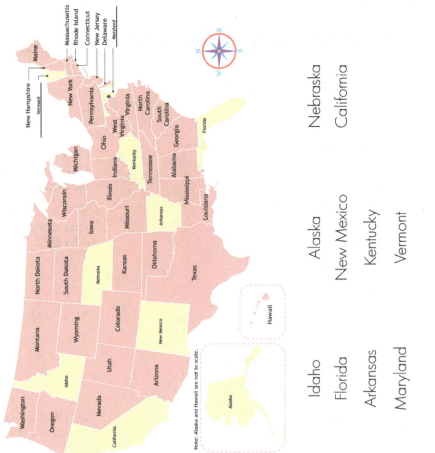

New York

Oregon

Colorado

Oklahoma

Maine

Louisiana

Illinois

South Carolina

Montana

West Virginia

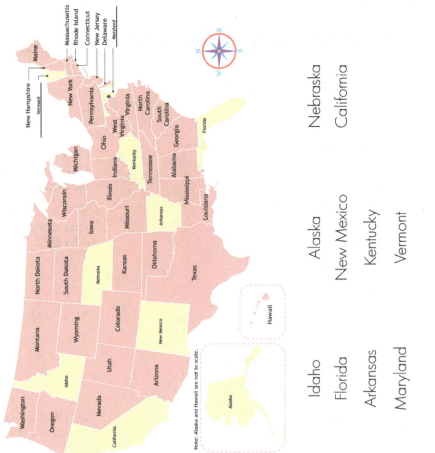

Name the States 2

The United States map is missing some of the names of its states! Use the word bank to help you fill in the names.

Idaho

Florida

Arkansas

Maryland

Alaska

New Mexico

Kentucky

Vermont

Nebraska

California

114

What's That State? 2

Use a map to help you identify the states by their shapes.
You can also use the state capitals as clues.

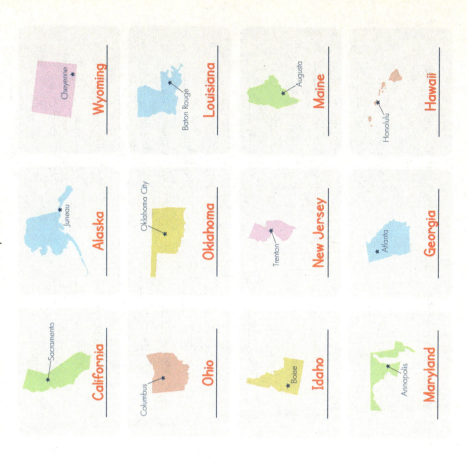

Sacramento — California

Columbus — Ohio

Boise — Idaho

Annapolis — Maryland

Juneau — Alaska

Oklahoma City — Oklahoma

Trenton — New Jersey

Atlanta — Georgia

Cheyenne — Wyoming

Baton Rouge — Louisiana

Augusta — Maine

Honolulu — Hawaii

What's That State? 1

Use a map to help you identify the states by their shapes.
You can also use the state capitals as clues.

Carson City — Nevada

Albany — New York

Springfield — Illinois

Richmond — Virginia

Austin — Texas

Salt Lake City — Utah

Nashville — Tennessee

Jefferson City — Missouri

Lincoln — Nebraska

Columbia — South Carolina

Montgomery — Alabama

Olympia — Washington

Make It Short!

Each state in the United States has its own two-letter postal abbreviation. Use the map on this page to find the postal abbreviation for every state.

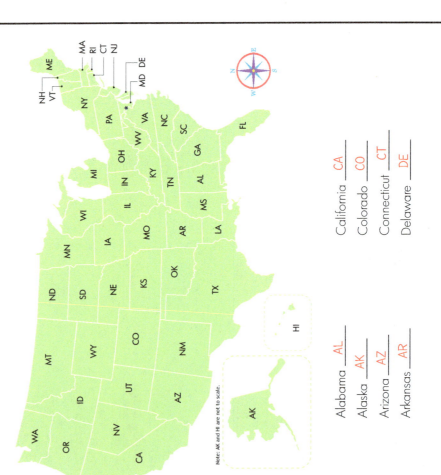

Note: AK and HI are not to scale.

Alabama ___AL___
Alaska ___AK___
Arizona ___AZ___
Arkansas ___AR___

California ___CA___
Colorado ___CO___
Connecticut ___CT___
Delaware ___DE___

Continue to write the postal abbreviation for every state.

Florida ___FL___
Georgia ___GA___
Hawaii ___HI___
Idaho ___ID___
Illinois ___IL___
Indiana ___IN___
Iowa ___IA___
Kansas ___KS___
Kentucky ___KY___
Louisiana ___LA___
Maine ___ME___
Maryland ___MD___
Massachusetts ___MA___
Michigan ___MI___
Minnesota ___MN___
Mississippi ___MS___
Missouri ___MO___
Montana ___MT___
Nebraska ___NE___
Nevada ___NV___
New Hampshire ___NH___

New Jersey ___NJ___
New Mexico ___NM___
New York ___NY___
North Carolina ___NC___
North Dakota ___ND___
Ohio ___OH___
Oklahoma ___OK___
Oregon ___OR___
Pennsylvania ___PA___
Rhode Island ___RI___
South Carolina ___SC___
South Dakota ___SD___
Tennessee ___TN___
Texas ___TX___
Utah ___UT___
Vermont ___VT___
Virginia ___VA___
Washington ___WA___
West Virginia ___WV___
Wisconsin ___WI___
Wyoming ___WY___

Scrambled States!

Unscramble the names of the states below. If you need a hint, take a look at the picture bank!

1. THSOU KDAOTA — SOUTH DAKOTA
2. CMIHGAIN — MICHIGAN
3. YKNETKUC — KENTUCKY
4. AUTH — UTAH
5. TEMOVRN — VERMONT
6. GANJIIVR — VIRGINIA
7. SMIUSRIO — MISSOURI
8. GEONOR — OREGON
9. IMEAN — MAINE
10. ABAALAM — ALABAMA
11. CISSIWNON — WISCONSIN
12. HRNTO RALOACIN — NORTH CAROLINA
13. EWN EYEJSR — NEW JERSEY
14. SKASAN — KANSAS
15. LSINIOIL — ILLINOIS
16. HAIDO — IDAHO
17. LDAFORI — FLORIDA
18. WNE CMIXOE — NEW MEXICO
19. YADARNLM — MARYLAND
20. GYMONIW — WYOMING
21. OEGGIAR — GEORGIA
22. SOAILIANU — LOUISIANA
23. TNCIOTCCEUN — CONNECTICUT
24. HIOO — OHIO
25. DOOLACRO — COLORADO

Picture Bank:

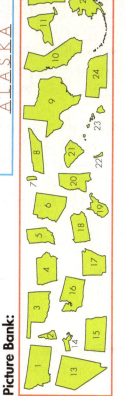

page 46

More Scrambled States!

Unscramble the names of the states below. If you need a hint, take a look at the picture bank!

1. NAMOANT — MONTANA
2. NVVE PHIMAHSER — NEW HAMPSHIRE
3. HOAMOALK — OKLAHOMA
4. WAIO — IOWA
5. DAIANIN — INDIANA
6. RZAINOA — ARIZONA
7. HEDOR ALSIDN — RHODE ISLAND
8. NESTEESEN — TENNESSEE
9. AXETS — TEXAS
10. FLACOINARI — CALIFORNIA
11. EWN KYOR — NEW YORK
12. STMINEANO — MINNESOTA
13. DANVAE — NEVADA
14. SACASHETUSTMS — MASSACHUSETTS
15. RNHOT KADOAT — NORTH DAKOTA
16. GOHIWANTSN — WASHINGTON
17. RASKAANS — ARKANSAS
18. YALNPNEVIANS — PENNSYLVANIA
19. STEW NGIIVAIR — WEST VIRGINIA
20. PSIPISIMSSI — MISSISSIPPI
21. UTSHO OCRAILAN — SOUTH CAROLINA
22. WEAREALD — DELAWARE
23. IHAIAW — HAWAII
24. BANEKASR — NEBRASKA
25. KASAAL — ALASKA

page 47

117

Extreme State Facts page 48

Match each extreme fact to its state!

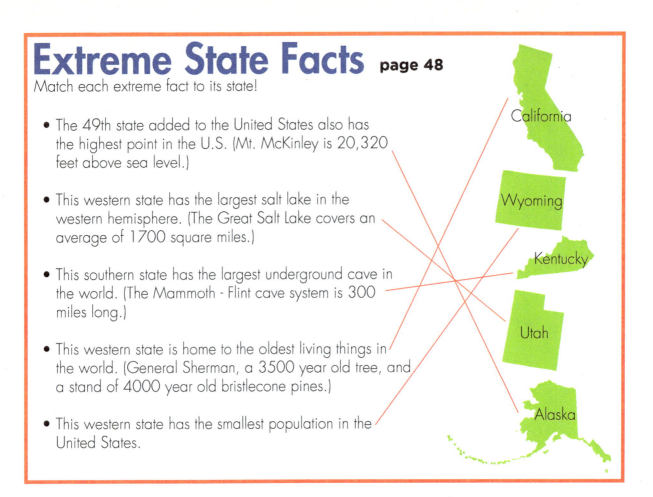

- The 49th state added to the United States also has the highest point in the U.S. (Mt. McKinley is 20,320 feet above sea level.)

- This western state has the largest salt lake in the western hemisphere. (The Great Salt Lake covers an average of 1700 square miles.)

- This southern state has the largest underground cave in the world. (The Mammoth - Flint cave system is 300 miles long.)

- This western state is home to the oldest living things in the world. (General Sherman, a 3500 year old tree, and a stand of 4000 year old bristlecone pines.)

- This western state has the smallest population in the United States.

California

Wyoming

Kentucky

Utah

Alaska

Notable State Facts page 49

Molly has collected her state facts, but can't remember which facts go with which states. Can you help her by drawing a line between the facts and their matching states?

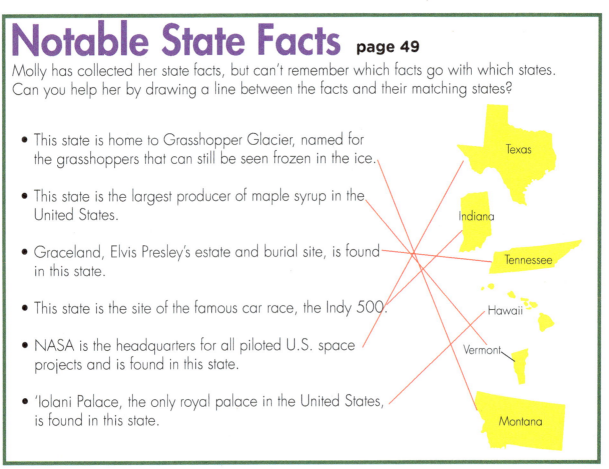

- This state is home to Grasshopper Glacier, named for the grasshoppers that can still be seen frozen in the ice.

- This state is the largest producer of maple syrup in the United States.

- Graceland, Elvis Presley's estate and burial site, is found in this state.

- This state is the site of the famous car race, the Indy 500.

- NASA is the headquarters for all piloted U.S. space projects and is found in this state.

- 'Iolani Palace, the only royal palace in the United States, is found in this state.

Texas

Indiana

Tennessee

Hawaii

Vermont

Montana

Going to the Coast page 50

Match each fact with its east coast state!

- The most easterly point in the United States, West Quoddy Head is found in this state.

- This state is where the Boston Tea Party occured in 1773.

- The first battle of the Civil War took place at Fort Sumter in this state.

- Noah Webster, the author of the first dictionary was born in this state in 1807.

- Known as the Venice of America, the city of Fort Lauderdale has 185 miles of local waterways and is found in this state.

Florida

Maine

Connecticut

Massachusetts

South Carolina

Launch Coordinates page 56

Casey is looking for the perfect place to launch his rocket ship. He has found 4 possible locations. Use the coordinates below to locate the 4 states that Casey can launch from.

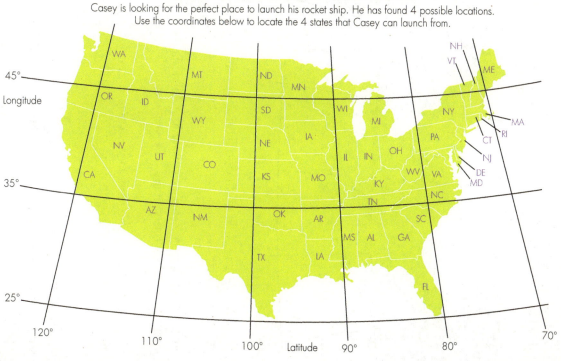

1. This location is at 30° north and 97° west: _Texas_

2. This location is at 41° north and 78° west: _Pennsylvania_

3. This location is at 39° north and 120° west: _California_

4. This location is at 46° north and 108° west: _Montana_

State Coordinates   page 57

Can you name the states located at the coordinates given below?

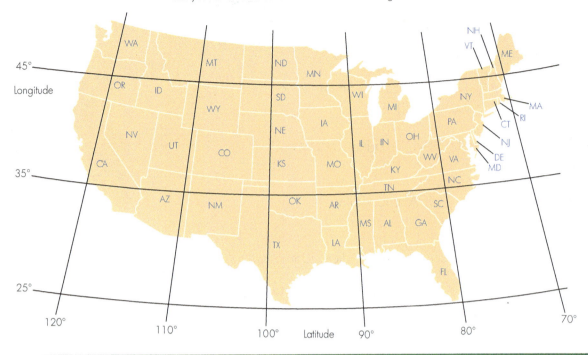

1. This location is at 37° north and 105° west: _Colorado_   2. This location is at 27° north and 82° west: _Florida_

3. This location is at 44° north and 75° west: _New York_   4. This location is at 38° north and 91° west: _Missouri_

State Scavenger Hunt

Zach and Ronnie are on a state scavenger hunt.
Use the clues below to help them find the states they're looking for!

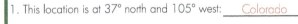

1. Start in Wyoming. Move one state north and then 3 states to the east. What state are you in?   _Wisconsin_

2. Start in Alabama. Move one state north. Follow the 35° latitude line west 4 states. What state are you in?   _New Mexico_

3. Start in east Michigan. Move to the state that is south and east. Move one state northeast. Then go one more state north. What state are you in?   _New York_

4. Start in South Dakota. Follow the 100° longitude line 2 states south. Go 2 states west. Then go to the bordering northwest state. What state are you in?   _Idaho_

page 58

Guess the Capital SCRAMBLE!

Get started by unscrambling the name of each state capital, then see if you can match it to its home state!

NHEELA	Helena
JEUUNA	Juneau
NNCLOLI	Lincoln
MNIROTPEEL	Montpelier
ORDNCCO	Concord
VDOER	Dover
UANSTI	Austin
XNHOEPI	Phoenix
ATSNA EF	Santa Fe
BEIOS	Boise
ARHILEG	Raleigh
HCARNSTLEO	Charleston
NEDSPRFILIG	Springfield

ILLINOIS
ARIZONA
TEXAS
IDAHO
NEW MEXICO
NORTH CAROLINA
NEW HAMPSHIRE
NEBRASKA
MONTANA
ALASKA
DELAWARE
WEST VIRGINIA
VERMONT

Up, Down, and All Around!

See if you can name the missing state capitals using the capital cities of the states that surround it as clues.
For example:

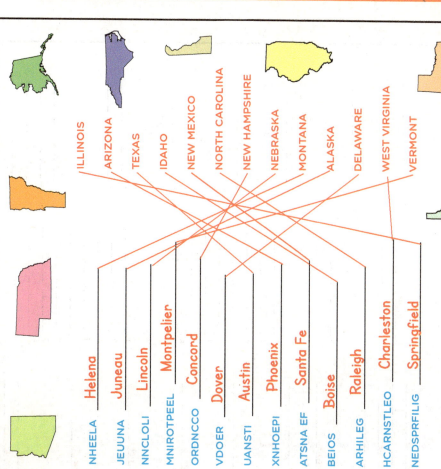

Salt Lake City: Carson City, Boise, Cheyenne, Denver, Santa Fe, Phoenix

THIS CAPITAL	IS BORDERED BY
Jefferson City, MO	: Topeka, Lincoln, Des Moines, Springfield,
	Frankfort, Nashville, Little Rock, Oklahoma City
Concord, NH	: Montpelier, Boston, Augusta
Austin, TX	: Santa Fe, Oklahoma City, Little Rock, Baton Rouge
Sacramento, CA	: Salem, Carson City, Phoenix
Tallahassee, FL	: Montgomery, Atlanta
Lansing, MI	: Indianapolis, Columbus
Harrisburg, PA	: Trenton, Dover, Annapolis, Charleston,
	Columbus, Albany
Helena, MT	: Boise, Cheyenne , Bismarck, Pierre
Columbia, SC	: Atlanta, Raleigh
St. Paul, MN	: Bismarck, Pierre, Des Moines, Madison

Alphabetical Order States

We've listed the number of states that start with a certain letter – see if you can name them all from memory! For more fun, print out a second copy and give one to a friend. Start a timer or a stopwatch and see who finishes first!

A
1. Alabama
2. Alaska
3. Arizona
4. Arkansas

C
1. California
2. Colorado
3. Connecticut

D
1. Delaware

F
1. Florida

G
1. Georgia

H
1. Hawaii

I
1. Idaho
2. Illinois
3. Indiana
4. Iowa

K
1. Kansas
2. Kentucky

L
1. Louisiana

M
1. Maine
2. Maryland
3. Massachusetts
4. Michigan
5. Minnesota
6. Mississippi
7. Missouri
8. Montana

N
1. Nebraska
2. Nevada
3. New Hampshire
4. New Jersey
5. New Mexico
6. New York
7. North Carolina
8. North Dakota

O
1. Ohio
2. Oklahoma
3. Oregon

P
1. Pennsylvania

R
1. Rhode Island

S
1. South Carolina
2. South Dakota

T
1. Tennessee
2. Texas

U
1. Utah

V
1. Vermont
2. Virginia

W
1. Washington
2. West Virginia
3. Wisconsin
4. Wyoming

FROM TO

page 75

CRACK THE CODE

We've listed every state and their capital in alphabetical order by state. See if you can name all the states and their capitals using only the first letter of every word to help you!

A Alabama : M Montgomery
A Alaska : J Juneau
A Arizona : P Phoenix
A Arkansas : L Little R Rock
C California : S Sacramento
C Colorado : D Denver
C Connecticut : H Hartford
D Delaware : D Dover
F Florida : T Tallahassee
G Georgia : A Atlanta
H Hawaii : H Honolulu
I Idaho : B Boise
I Illinois : S Springfield
I Indiana : I Indianapolis
I Iowa : D Des M Moines
K Kansas : T Topeka
K Kentucky : F Frankfurt
L Louisiana : B Baton R Rouge
M Maine : A Augusta
M Maryland : A Annapolis
M Massachusetts : B Boston
M Michigan : L Lansing
M Minnesota : S St. P Paul
M Mississippi : J Jackson
M Missouri : J Jefferson C City
M Montana : H Helena

page 96

CRACK THE CODE

We've listed every state and their capital in alphabetical order by state. See if you can name all the states and their capitals using only the first letter of every word to help you!

N _Nebraska_ : L _Lincoln_

N _Nevada_ : C _Carson_ C _City_

N _New_ H _Hampshire_ : C _Concord_

N _New_ J _Jersey_ : T _Trenton_

N _New_ M _Mexico_ : S _Santa_ F _Fe_

N _New_ Y _York_ : A _Albany_

N _North_ C _Carolina_ : R _Raleigh_

N _North_ D _Dakota_ : B _Bismark_

O _Ohio_ : C _Columbus_

O _Oklahoma_ : O _Oklahoma_ C _City_

O _Oregon_ : S _Salem_

P _Pennsylvania_ : H _Harrisburg_

R _Rhode_ I _Island_ : P _Providence_

S _South_ C _Carolina_ : C _Columbia_

S _South_ D _Dakota_ : P _Pierre_

T _Tennessee_ : N _Nashville_

T _Texas_ : A _Austin_

U _Utah_ : S _Salt_ L _Lake_ C _City_

V _Vermont_ : M _Montpelier_

V _Virginia_ : R _Richmond_

W _Washington_ : O _Olympia_

W _West_ V _Virginia_ : C _Charleston_

W _Wisconsin_ : M _Madison_

W _Wyoming_ : C _Cheyenne_

page 97